# CHEESECAKES

Edited by
Rhona Newman

# CONTENTS

This edition first published 1978 by
Octopus Books Limited
59 Grosvenor Street, London W.1.

© 1978 Octopus Books Limited

Reprinted 1980

ISBN 0 7064 0664 8

Produced and printed in Hong Kong by
Mandarin Publishers Limited
22a Westlands Road, Quarry Bay

*Frontispiece:* COFFEE AND BRANDY CHEESECAKE *(page 90)*,
GINGER CHEESECAKE *(page 86) (Photograph: Kraft Foods)*

# Weights and Measures

All measurements in this book are based on Imperial weights and measures, with American equivalents given in parenthesis.

Measurements in *weight* in the Imperial and American system are the same. Measurements in *volume* are different, and the following table shows the equivalents:

**Spoon measurements**

| Imperial | U.S. |
|---|---|
| 1 tablespoon | 1 tablespoon |
| 1½ tablespoons | 2 tablespoons |
| 2 tablespoons | 3 tablespoons |
| | (abbrev: T) |

Level spoon measurements are used in all the recipes.

**Liquid measurements**

| | |
|---|---|
| 1 Imperial pint | 20 fluid ounces |
| 1 American pint | 16 fluid ounces |
| 1 American cup | 8 fluid ounces |

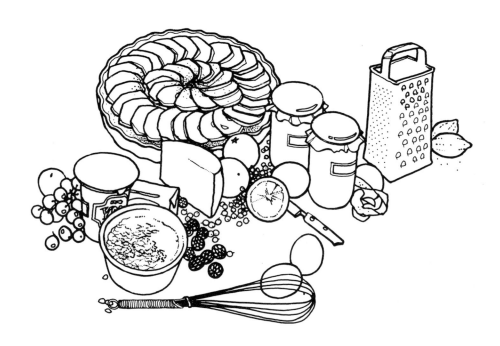

# INTRODUCTION

Very few people can resist the temptation of a piece of cheesecake when it is offered. The smooth creamy texture contrasted with the sharpness of lemon or other fruit is deliciously satisfying.

Cheesecakes are now becoming increasingly popular everywhere whether served as a dessert, teatime gâteau or mid morning treat. Apart from looking attractive and tasting good, cheesecakes have the added advantage that they can be prepared well in advance and left to chill in a refrigerator. Furthermore, all types of cheesecake will freeze very well.

The cheesecake as it is known today, is a comparatively recent recipe. It originated from the traditional Yorkshire Cheesecake which was made from a local curd cheese, eggs and lemon, then baked in a pastry case.

Lemon is the flavour mostly associated with cheesecakes as it aids setting and gives a pleasant sharpness. However, it is not essential and there are many alternatives that can be used. Flavours such as coffee, chocolate and ginger combine well with the ingredients used in cheesecakes.

There are a few basic types of cheesecake but these can have an endless variety of textures, flavours and toppings. The cheesecake which requires baking is usually heavier and richer than the lighter gelatine set type which is often called an American cheesecake. A softer texture can be achieved by omitting gelatine and allowing the filling to become firm with chilling. It is therefore, important to serve this variety of cheesecake straight from the refrigerator.

Cheese, usually soft, is the essential ingredient in all cheesecakes. As there are several kinds of soft cheese with varying fat contents this will determine the richness and texture of the cheesecake.

The filling can be further enriched by the addition of cream; this may be included as double (heavy), single (light), soured cream or a combination of two. Whipped double (heavy) cream is often used as part of the decoration to make the cheesecake more attractive and tempting. Many recipes include yogurt to give extra flavour and piquancy, but as an alternative to cream it makes a less rich cheesecake.

Most cheesecakes include eggs which can be used whole, beaten with other ingredients, or separated, the whites being whisked and folded in to give a lighter filling.

A less moist cheesecake results with the addition of flour or cornflour to the filling; this is particularly important in the baked varieties. Ground rice can be substituted to give a rougher texture or for a more expensive cheesecake ground almonds give a special flavour.

As well as variations in cheesecake fillings there are many different bases. The most popular is the biscuit crumb which may have additional ingredients and flavourings. The pastry and sponge bases are more usual in the traditional baked cheesecakes.

Finally the toppings and decorations for cheesecakes can provide endless variety. Fruit is the most popular, adding not only flavour but colour and texture. Fresh fruit toppings can be selected according to the season. In summer choose delicious strawberries, raspberries and blackcurrants. At Christmas when soft fruit is expensive, use citrus fruits: oranges, lemons and grapefruit.

For those about to discover cheesecakes this book gives both traditional and new ideas. For those already addicted here is the opportunity to extend your repertoire of cheesecake recipes.

CHERRY CHEESECAKE *(page 34),* WALNUT AND ORANGE CHEESECAKE *(page 62),* LEMON AND SULTANA CHEESECAKE *(page 27) (Photograph: National Dairy Council)*

# Freezing Cheesecakes

All cheesecakes freeze very well whether cooked, gelatine set or the chilled variety. Best results are obtained if the cheesecake is made without the topping and frozen uncovered. When it is hard it can be wrapped and sealed until required. Before thawing the cheesecake the wrapping should be removed. It can then be left at room temperature to soften. This will take 3-4 hours for baked cheesecakes and 2-3 hours for gelatine set or chilled cheesecakes. Alternatively all cheesecakes can be thawed in a refrigerator overnight. Toppings and decorations can then be added as required before serving.

# Soft Cheeses

There are many soft cream cheeses available; although these may have a variety of names they should include a description to indicate the fat content. As the cheesecake recipes in this book use a selection of cheeses the following descriptions may help to avoid confusion.

**Full fat soft cheese** — must contain a minimum of 20% milk fat and a maximum of 60% water. However, the average is 80% milk fat which will give a rich cheesecake. Where a recipe states full fat soft cheese it should be used to give a good result.

**Medium fat soft cheese** — must contain between 10-20% milk fat with not more than 70% water. This is often·sold as curd cheese as well as medium fat soft cheese; it is suitable for most cheesecake recipes.

**Low fat soft cheese** — must contain between 2-10% milk fat and not more than 80% water. This is sold as low fat curd cheese and will give a lighter cheesecake unless extra cream is added. Quark is the German name given to this cheese and Ricotta is the Italian equivalent.

**Skimmed milk soft cheese (cottage cheese)** — must contain less than 2% milk fat and not more than 80% water. It is made from pasteurized fat free milk and has a characteristic granular texture. Cottage cheese will give a light cheesecake and is best sieved before mixing with other ingredients.

Where a recipe states 'cream cheese' a full fat or medium fat cheese will give the best result.

**Curd cheese** — is prepared from milk soured naturally. It is available in most delicatessens and large supermarkets but if you can obtain non-pasteurized milk from a local dairy or farm try making your own.

Pour 2 pints (5 cups) milk into a large bowl and stir in 1 tablespoon natural (unflavored) yogurt. Leave in a warm place overnight or until soft curd has formed.

Place the curd in a piece of muslin or cheesecloth and tie to form a small bag. Hang this over a bowl and allow to drain for 12-16 hours or until the curd is firm but not dry and crumbly. Remove the curd from the bag and place in a bowl. Beat thoroughly until smooth and add salt to taste.

Use the curd on the same day for making cheesecakes or store in a refrigerator for up to 24 hours. This quantity of milk will yield approximately 4 oz. (½ cup) curd cheese.

# BAKED CHEESECAKES

## Orange Cheesecake Pie

**Shortcrust pastry (basic pie dough) base:**
4 oz. (1 cup) plain (all-purpose) flour
¼ teaspoon salt
1 oz. (2T) butter
1 oz. (2T) lard (shortening)
4 teaspoons cold water (approximately)
**Filling:**
12 oz. (1½ cups) cream cheese

2 eggs
4 oz. (½ cup) castor (superfine) sugar
1 small can frozen concentrated orange juice, defrosted
**Topping:**
1 oz. (2T) castor (superfine) sugar
1 oz. (¼ cup) flour
4 oz. (1 cup) canned crushed pineapple, drained

Sift the flour and salt into a bowl. Cut the fat into small pieces and rub into the flour using the fingertips until the mixture resembles fine breadcrumbs. Add enough water to mix to a firm dough. Roll out thinly on a floured board.

Use the pastry to line an 8 inch flan dish. Bake 'blind' at 425°F, Gas Mark 7 for 15 minutes. Remove from the oven and allow to cool.

Soften cream cheese in a bowl and beat in eggs and sugar. Mix in half the orange juice and pour into pastry case. Bake at 250°F, Gas Mark ½ for 30-40 minutes until firm.

Make up remaining orange juice to ¼ pint (⅔ cup) with water. Blend with sugar and flour for the topping. Heat, stirring continuously, and boil for 1 minute. Stir in crushed pineapple and spread over the hot pie. Chill for 8 hours.
**Serves 8-10**

# Baked Hazelnut and Strawberry Cheesecake

**Base:**
4 oz. (1 cup) hazelnut (filbert) biscuits, crushed
**Filling:**
1½ lb. (3 cups) Quark cheese
4 eggs, separated
6 oz. (¾ cup) castor (superfine) sugar
1 tablespoon cornflour (cornstarch)
1 lemon, grated rind and juice
½ teaspoon vanilla essence
¼ pint (⅔ cup) double (heavy) cream, whipped
**Topping:**
¼ pint (⅔ cup) double (heavy) cream, whipped
strawberries

Cover the base of a greased 9 inch loose bottomed cake tin with crushed biscuits.

Place Quark in a bowl and beat in egg yolks. Add sugar, cornflour, lemon rind, juice and vanilla essence and mix well. Fold in the whipped cream. Whisk egg whites until stiff and fold into the mixture. Place in the tin and smooth the top. Bake at 300°F, Gas Mark 2 for 1½ hours. Leave to cool in the oven for 1½ hours with heat off and door ajar. Remove from tin and decorate with whipped cream and strawberries. Chill before serving.
**Serves 12**

# Nutty Lemon Cheesecake

**Base:**
2 oz. (¼ cup) butter
6 oz. (3 cups) fresh breadcrumbs
2 oz. (¼ cup) castor (superfine) sugar
1½ teaspoons cinnamon
**Filling:**
3 eggs, separated
4 oz. (½ cup) castor (superfine) sugar
12 oz. (1½ cups) cottage cheese, sieved
1 lemon, grated rind and juice
¼ pint (⅔ cup) single (light) cream
**Topping:**
1 oz. (3T) nuts, chopped

Melt butter in a large shallow pan and add breadcrumbs. Stir occasionally while heating until lightly browned. Mix in sugar and cinnamon. Leave to cool.

Grease the base and sides of an 8 inch tin and press two-thirds of the crumb mixture into the base of the tin.

Place egg yolks in a bowl and beat in sugar until creamy. Blend in cottage cheese, lemon rind, juice and cream. Whisk egg whites lightly and fold into the mixture. Pour into the tin and bake at 325°F, Gas Mark 3 for 50 minutes. Sprinkle remaining breadcrumb mixture and chopped nuts over the cheesecake. Continue cooking for a further 15-25 minutes. Leave to cool in the tin. Chill before serving.
**Serves 8**

BAKED HAZELNUT AND STRAWBERRY CHEESECAKE
*(Photograph: CMA UK)*

# Apple Cheesecake

**Base:**
4 oz. (1 cup) self-raising flour
pinch of salt
1 oz. (2T) butter
1 oz. (2T) lard
½ oz. (1T) castor (superfine) sugar
**Filling:**
12 oz. (3 cups) cooking apples,
  peeled, cored and stewed

8 oz. (1 cup) curd cheese
½ oz. (2T) custard powder
2 oz. (¼ cup) castor (superfine)
  sugar
1 large egg, separated
**Topping:**
icing (confectioners') sugar, sifted

Sift flour and salt into a bowl and rub in butter and lard until the mixture resembles fine breadcrumbs. Stir in sugar. Bind with approximately 1 tablespoon cold water to make a stiff dough. Roll pastry to line an 8 inch fluted flan tin.

Drain excess liquid from the stewed apples and place in the base of the pastry case.

Beat the curd cheese with the custard powder, sugar and egg yolk. Whisk the egg white until stiff and fold into the mixture. Spread over the apples. Bake at 375°F, Gas Mark 5 for 30-35 minutes. Cool and serve dusted with sifted icing sugar.
**Serves 6**

# Layer Cheesecake

**Base:**
2 oz. (¼ cup) butter, melted
4 oz. (1 cup) digestive biscuits
  (graham crackers), crushed
1 teaspoon cinnamon
finely grated rind of 1 lemon
**Filling:**
8 oz. (1 cup) cottage cheese,
  sieved

2 eggs, beaten
2 oz. (¼ cup) castor (superfine)
  sugar
few drops of vanilla essence
**Topping:**
¼ pint (⅔ cup) soured cream
fresh or canned apricot or peach
  halves

Mix butter, biscuits, cinnamon and lemon rind. Press into an 8 inch flan ring on a baking tray. Leave to cool.

Mix cottage cheese, eggs, sugar and vanilla essence. Pour onto biscuit base. Bake at 375°F, Gas Mark 5 for 20 minutes. Remove cheesecake from the oven and spread soured cream over the top. Return to the oven for 5 minutes.

When cool decorate with fresh or canned fruit. Serve chilled.
**Serves 6**
The soured cream sets on cooking to give the cheesecake a refreshing, piquant flavour.

# Rum and Raisin Cheesecake

**Filling:**
5 oz. (⅔ cup) butter
5 oz. (⅔ cup) cream cheese
5 oz. (⅔ cup) castor (superfine) sugar
5 oz. (1¼ cups) ground almonds
5 eggs, separated
1 miniature bottle rum
4 oz. (⅔ cup) raisins

**Topping:**
½ pint (1¼ cups) double (heavy) cream
2 fresh dates, halved
1 oz. (3T) sultanas
1 oz. (3T) raisins
1 oz. (3T) currants
1 oz. (¼ cup) flaked almonds, browned

Grease and line an 8 inch loose bottomed cake tin. Cream together the butter and cream cheese. Add sugar, ground almonds, egg yolks and rum. Mix well and stir in the raisins. Whisk egg whites until very stiff and fold into mixture.

Spoon into the tin and bake at 400°F, Gas Mark 6 for 15 minutes, then reduce temperature to 350°F, Gas Mark 4 for a further 45 minutes until the cheesecake is golden brown and dry inside when tested with a skewer. (If the cake browns too quickly, cover with a double sheet of greaseproof (waxed) paper). Cool cheesecake and remove from the tin.

Whip the cream until thick and pipe a little into each date half. Decorate the top edge of the cheesecake with piped cream rosettes and spread the remaining cream around the sides of the cheesecake. Press on the dried fruit and browned almonds. Arrange the stuffed dates on top of the cheesecake. Chill before serving.

**Serves 6-8**

# Cooked Pineapple Cheesecake

**Base:**
2 oz. (¼ cup) soft margarine
4 oz. (1 cup) digestive biscuits
  (graham crackers), crushed
2 oz. (¼ cup) sugar
2 oz. (½ cup) walnuts, chopped
**Filling:**
15½ oz. can pineapple rings
8 oz. (1 cup) full fat soft cheese

2 oz. (¼ cup) sugar
2 eggs, separated
1 oz. (¼ cup) flour, sifted
**Topping:**
¼ pint (⅔ cup) soured cream
2 oz. (¼ cup) castor (superfine)
  sugar
whipped cream to decorate
1 biscuit, crushed

Melt margarine and mix with biscuits, sugar and walnuts. Press into the base of an 8-9 inch greased fluted flan tin with removable base.

Drain pineapple rings and reserve 1 tablespoon juice. Blend the juice with the cheese. Gradually add sugar and egg yolks, beating thoroughly. Reserve 2 pineapple rings for decoration and chop the remainder. Mix into cheese mixture with the flour. Whisk egg whites until stiff and fold in. Pour over biscuit base and bake at 350°F, Gas Mark 4 for 1 hour.

Mix the soured cream with the sugar. Remove cheesecake from the oven and spread the topping over. Bake at 300°F, Gas Mark 2 for a further 15 minutes. Cool then remove from the tin.

Decorate the top of the cheesecake with the reserved pineapple and whirls of cream. Sprinkle biscuit crumbs over the cream. Serve chilled.
**Serves 8-10**

# Continental Cheesecake

**Base:**
2 oz. (¼ cup) soft margarine
2 oz. (¼ cup) self-raising flour
½ teaspoon baking powder
2 oz. (¼ cup) castor (superfine)
  sugar
**Filling:**
3 oz. (⅓ cup) soft margarine
2 oz. (¼ cup) castor (superfine)
  sugar

1 lemon, juice and grated rind
1 egg
2 oz. (½ cup) plain (all-purpose)
  flour, sifted
2 oz. (⅓ cup) sultanas
1 lb. (2 cups) full fat soft cheese
½ pint (1¼ cups) double (heavy)
  cream

Place margarine, flour, baking powder and sugar in a bowl. Beat together for 1-2 minutes until smooth and creamy. Spread over the base of a greased 8 inch loose bottomed cake tin.

Cream together the margarine, sugar and lemon rind until light and fluffy. Gradually beat in the egg and lemon juice. Fold in the flour and sultanas. In a separate bowl soften the cheese and gradually blend in the cream, mixing well. Fold into the mixture until smooth. Pour over base and bake at 325°F, Gas Mark 3 for 1¼-1½ hours. Allow to cool.

Remove the tin but leave cheesecake on base. Chill before serving.
**Serves 10-12**

CONTINENTAL CHEESECAKE, LEMON REFRIGERATED
CHEESECAKE *(page 67)*, COOKED PINEAPPLE CHEESECAKE
*(Photograph: Kraft Foods)*

# Lattice Cheesecake

**Base:**
8 oz. (2 cups) plain (all-purpose)
  flour
pinch of salt
4 oz. (½ cup) butter
1½ oz. (3T) castor (superfine)
  sugar
1 egg yolk
2 tablespoons (3T) water

**Filling:**
4 eggs
2 oz. (¼ cup) sugar
1 lemon, juice and grated rind
8 oz. (1 cup) cottage cheese,
  sieved
½ pint (1¼ cups) soured cream
½ oz. (2T) flour
1½ oz. (4½T) currants
2 oz. (⅓ cup) candied peel

Sift flour and salt into a bowl and rub in butter until the mixture resembles fine breadcrumbs. Stir in sugar. Mix egg yolk with water and use to bind the dough. Cover and chill for 1 hour.

Roll the pastry thinly on a floured surface to a diameter of 12 inches. Place in an 8 inch loose bottomed cake tin. Trim so that pastry comes only 1¾ inches up the sides of the tin. Bake 'blind' at 400°F, Gas Mark 6 for 20 minutes. Roll out trimmings and remaining pastry and cut into ¼ inch strips for the lattice decoration.

Beat together the eggs and sugar. Add lemon juice, grated rind, cottage cheese, soured cream, flour, currants and candied peel. Mix thoroughly and pour into the pastry case. Bake at 350°F, Gas Mark 4 for 25 minutes. Arrange the strips of pastry in a lattice pattern over the top and return to the oven for a further 20 minutes. Turn off heat and leave cheesecake to cool in the oven.
**Serves 8**

# Black Cherry Cheesecake

**Base:**
3 oz. (¾ cup) flour, sifted
2 oz. (¼ cup) butter
1 oz. (2T) castor (superfine) sugar
**Filling:**
3 oz. (¼ cup) black (bing) cherry
  jam
4 oz. (½ cup) cottage cheese,
  sieved

1½ oz. (3T) castor (superfine)
  sugar
1 oz. (¼ cup) cornflour
  (cornstarch)
2 eggs, beaten
¼ pint (⅔ cup) double (heavy)
  cream

Place flour, butter and sugar in a bowl. Rub together until the mixture resembles breadcrumbs. Knead together and roll shortbread to line the base of a shallow 8 inch tin. Spread the jam over the shortbread.

Blend together the cottage cheese, sugar, cornflour and eggs. Whip cream until thick and fold into the mixture. Spread over the jam and bake at 400°F, Gas Mark 6 for about 20 minutes or until firm. Serve cold.
**Serves 6**

18

# Apricot and Raisin Cheesecake

**Base:**
2 oz. (¼ cup) soft margarine
2 oz. (¼ cup) castor (superfine)
  sugar
1 egg
2 oz. (½ cup) self-raising flour
½ teaspoon baking powder

**Filling:**
12 oz. (1½ cups) cottage cheese,
  sieved
¼ pint (⅔ cup) double (heavy)
  cream
1 oz. (⅓ cup) desiccated
  (shredded) coconut

1 oz. (¼ cup) plain (all-purpose)
  flour
2 oz. (¼ cup) sugar
3 eggs, beaten
3 oz. (½ cup) dried apricots, finely
  chopped
1 oz. (3T) raisins

**Decoration:**
1 tablespoon (1T) icing
  (confectioners') sugar, sifted
2 tablespoons (3T) apricot jam
1 packet sponge finger (lady
  finger) biscuits

Place margarine, sugar, egg, flour and baking powder in a bowl and beat for 2-3 minutes. Pour into a greased and lined 7 inch square cake tin. Bake at 325°F, Gas Mark 3 for 15 minutes or until firm.

Mix cottage cheese, cream, coconut, flour, sugar, eggs, apricots and raisins and pour over sponge base. Return to the oven for 1¼ hours. Turn off oven and leave cheesecake for a further 30 minutes.

Remove from the oven, take out of the tin and place on a serving plate. Dredge top of cake with icing sugar. Warm and sieve apricot jam and use to brush the sides of cake. Cut sponge fingers (lady fingers) in half and arrange with rounded sides uppermost along sides of cake.
**Serves 12**

# Austrian Cheesecake

**Base:**
2 oz. (½ cup) digestive biscuits
 (graham crackers), crushed
**Filling:**
1 lb. (2 cups) cottage cheese,
 sieved
¼ pint (⅔ cup) milk
2 eggs, separated

2 oz. (½ cup) cornflour
 (cornstarch)
5 oz. (⅔ cup) sugar
1 teaspoon vanilla essence
**Topping:**
whipped cream
fresh raspberries

Sprinkle crushed biscuits in the bottom of a greased 9 inch loose based cake tin.

Place cottage cheese, milk, egg yolks and cornflour in a bowl and mix well. Whisk egg whites until stiff and fold into mixture together with the sugar and vanilla essence. Pour over biscuit crumbs and bake at 350°F, Gas Mark 4 for 30-35 minutes. Cool and remove from tin. Decorate with whipped cream and fresh raspberries.
**Serves 6**

# Baked Blender Cheesecake

**Base:**
8 oz. (2 cups) digestive biscuits
 (graham crackers)
2 oz. (¼ cup) castor (superfine)
 sugar
4 oz. (½ cup) butter, melted
**Filling:**
½ pint (1 ¼ cups) milk
1 tablespoon lemon juice

4 eggs
5 oz. (⅔ cup) castor (superfine)
 sugar
1 oz. (¼ cup) flour
¼ teaspoon salt
1 lb. (2 cups) cottage cheese
**Topping:**
icing (confectioners') sugar

Crumble biscuits with sugar in an electric blender, then mix with melted butter. Press half the mixture into the base of a greased 8 inch loose based spring release cake tin.

Place all the ingredients for the filling in the goblet and mix until well blended. Pour over crumb base. Bake at 325°F, Gas Mark 3 for 1-1¼ hours until the centre is firm.

Cover with the remaining crumb mixture. Chill and remove from the tin. Cut 6 strips of greaseproof paper 1 inch wide and place in a lattice pattern over the cheesecake. Dust with sifted icing sugar, then carefully remove paper strips.
**Serves 8-10**
A quickly made cheesecake if a blender is available. Ingredients can be mixed by hand if no blender is available; this will give a slightly less smooth texture.

# Honey and Coconut Cheesecake

**Base:**
2 oz. (¼ cup) butter
2 oz. (¼ cup) castor (superfine) sugar
1½ oz. (⅓ cup) flour
3 oz. (1 cup) desiccated (shredded) coconut

**Filling:**
2 eggs, separated
2 oz. (3T) honey
1 oz. (¼ cup) cornflour (cornstarch)

½ teaspoon cinnamon
½ pint (1¼ cups) milk
8 oz. (1 cup) cottage cheese, sieved
¼ pint (⅔ cup) double (heavy) cream

**Topping:**
¼ pint (⅔ cup) double (heavy) cream
1 oz. (⅓ cup) desiccated (shredded) coconut

Cream butter and sugar together until light and fluffy. Mix in flour and coconut. Press the mixture to the base and sides of a buttered 8 inch sponge tin. Chill for 30 minutes then bake at 350°F, Gas Mark 4 for about 20 minutes until golden brown. Cool.

Mix egg yolks, honey, cornflour and cinnamon thoroughly together. Heat the milk and stir into the egg mixture. Return the mixture to the saucepan and cook stirring continuously until it thickens.

Allow to cool, then fold in the cottage cheese. Whip the cream until it stands in soft peaks and whisk the egg whites until stiff. Fold both into the cheese mixture and pour into the coconut case.

To decorate, whip the cream until thick and pipe a lattice pattern over the top. Toast the coconut until golden brown and sprinkle into the hollows of the lattice. Serve chilled.

**Serves 6-8**

This is a soft cheesecake and does not set as firmly as other varieties.

# Yorkshire Cheesecake

**Rich shortcrust pastry (pie dough) base:**
8 oz. (2 cups) plain (all-purpose) flour
pinch of salt
5 oz. (⅔ cup) butter
1 oz. (2T) castor (superfine) sugar
1 egg yolk
2 tablespoons (3T) water

**Filling:**
3 oz. (⅔ cup) currants
8 oz. (1 cup) cottage cheese, sieved
½ pint (1¼ cups) soured cream
2 oz. (¼ cup) castor (superfine) sugar
2 eggs
1 egg white
finely grated rind of 1 lemon

To make pastry base, sift flour and salt into a bowl and rub in the butter until mixture resembles fine breadcrumbs. Stir in the sugar. Blend egg yolk with water and use to bind mixture together. Chill for 30 minutes.

Roll out pastry to line a 10 inch flan dish or tin. Prick base and chill. Scatter currants over the pastry base. Mix together the cottage cheese, soured cream, sugar, eggs, egg white and lemon rind until well blended. Pour into pastry case.

Bake at 425°F, Gas Mark 7 for 10 minutes, then reduce temperature to 325°F, Gas Mark 3 for 20 minutes or until the cheesecake is firm. Serve cold.

**Serves 12**


# Traditional Cheesecake

**Base:**
4 oz. (1 cup) self-raising flour, sieved
2½ oz. (¼ cup + 1T) butter
1 oz. (¼ cup) icing (confectioners') sugar
1 egg yolk

**Filling:**
2 oz. (¼ cup) butter
3 oz. (⅓ cup) sugar
2 eggs, separated
1½ oz. (⅓ cup) ground almonds
1 oz. (2T) semolina
8 oz. (1 cup) cream cheese
1 lemon, grated rind and juice

Place flour in a bowl and rub in butter until the mixture resembles fine breadcrumbs. Stir in icing (confectioners') sugar. Bind together with the egg yolk and chill for 30 minues. Roll out pastry to line an 8 inch tin or dish.

Cream butter and sugar together. Add egg yolks, ground almonds, semolina, cream cheese, lemon rind and juice and mix thoroughly. Whisk egg whites until stiff and fold into the mixture. Pour into pastry case. Bake at 350°F, Gas Mark 4 for 50 minutes until the filling is set. If browning too quickly lower the oven temperature.

Cool before serving.

**Serves 6**

# Baked Orange and Sultana Cheesecake

**Base:**
4 oz. shortcrust pastry (basic pie
  dough), see page 11
**Filling:**
1 lb. (2 cups) curd cheese
1 oz. (¼ cup) flour
2 oz. (¼ cup) castor (superfine)
  sugar

2 eggs, beaten
2 tablespoons (3T) sweetened
  orange syrup
4 tablespoons (⅓ cup) soured
  cream
3 oz. (½ cup) sultanas
**Topping:**
sweetened orange syrup

Roll the pastry to line an 8 inch flan tin or dish. Beat curd cheese until
smooth, then blend in the flour, sugar, beaten eggs, orange syrup and
soured cream. Stir in the sultanas and pour mixture into the pastry case.
Level the top and bake at 350°F, Gas Mark 4 for approximately 1 hour.
Remove from the oven and glaze with orange syrup.
  Serve cold.
**Serves 6**

# Galliano Cheesecake

**Base:**
5 oz. (1 ¼ cups) plain (all-purpose)
  flour
2 oz. (¼ cup) sugar
½ teaspoon salt
½ teaspoon grated lemon rind
4 oz. (½ cup) butter
1 egg yolk
2 tablespoons (3T) Liquore
  Galliano

**Filling:**
2 lb. (4 cups) cottage cheese,
  sieved
4 eggs
4 oz. (½ cup) sugar
1 oz. (¼ cup) flour
3 tablespoons (¼ cup) Liquore
  Galliano
1 ½ tablespoons (2T) raisins
1 ½ tablespoons (2T) candied
  lemon peel, chopped

Sift flour into a bowl with sugar, salt and lemon peel. Rub in butter until the
mixture resembles fine breadcrumbs. Bind pastry together with egg yolk
and Galliano. Chill for 30 minutes. Roll pastry to line a 9 inch flan dish.
Bake 'blind' at 350°F, Gas Mark 4 for 15 minutes.
  Blend cottage cheese, eggs, sugar and flour in a bowl. Stir in Galliano,
raisins and candied lemon peel. Place in baked pastry case and bake at
325°F, Gas Mark 3 for 1 hour or until firm. Remove from oven and cool.
**Serves 8**
Liquore Galliano is an Italian herb based liqueur. If unobtainable substitute
Strega.

BAKED ORANGE AND SULTANA CHEESECAKE *(Photograph:
Delrosa)*

# Belgian Cheese Tart

**Base:**
7½ oz. packet frozen puff pastry
  (puff paste), thawed
**Filling:**
8 oz. (1 cup) cream cheese
2 eggs, beaten
¼ pint (⅔ cup) double (heavy)
  cream

½ lemon, grated rind and juice
1½ oz. (3T) castor (superfine)
  sugar
**Topping:**
icing (confectioners') sugar

Roll pastry thinly on a floured surface and line an 8 inch flan ring placed on a baking tray. Prick base thoroughly. Chill for 30 minutes then bake 'blind' at 425°F, Gas Mark 7 for 15 minutes.

Soften cheese and gradually beat in the eggs until smooth. Stir in the cream, lemon rind, juice and sugar without beating. Pour into the pastry case. Bake at 350°F, Gas Mark 4 for 25 minutes until the filling is set.

Allow to cool and then dust with sifted icing sugar. Serve cold.
**Serves 4-6**

# Dutch Lemon Cheesecake

**Base:**
6 oz. (1½ cups) plain (all-purpose)
  flour
pinch of salt
3 oz. (⅓ cup) butter
1½ tablespoons (2T) water
**Filling:**
6 oz. (1½ cups) Gouda cheese,
  grated
1 oz. (¼ cup) flour
3 tablespoons (¼ cup) single
  (light) cream

1 lemon, grated rind and juice
2 oz. (⅓ cup) sultanas
2 eggs, separated
3 oz. (⅓ cup) castor (superfine)
  sugar
**Topping:**
icing (confectioners') sugar, sifted
1 lemon, sliced
11 oz. can mandarin oranges,
  drained

Sift the flour and salt into a bowl and rub in the butter until the mixture resembles fine breadcrumbs. Bind together with water and knead with fingertips. Roll pastry to line an 8 inch fluted flan ring placed on a baking tray. Prick base with a fork and bake 'blind' at 425°F, Gas Mark 7 for 15 minutes. Cool.

Mix together the Gouda cheese, flour, cream, lemon rind, juice and sultanas. Beat the egg yolks and sugar together and add to the mixture. Whisk the egg whites until stiff and fold in.

Pour into flan case and bake at 350°F, Gas Mark 4 for 40-50 minutes. Cool and decorate with icing sugar, lemon slices and mandarins. Serve chilled with fresh cream.
**Serves 4-6**

# Lemon and Sultana Cheesecake

**Base:**
4 oz. shortcrust pastry (basic pie
  dough), see page 11
**Filling:**
1 lemon
6 oz. (¾ cup) cream cheese

2 oz. (¼ cup) castor (superfine)
  sugar
2 oz. (⅓ cup) sultanas
3 eggs, separated
**Topping:**
fresh lemon slices

Roll the pastry to line an 8 inch flan ring on a baking tray. Grate the rind
and squeeze the juice from the lemon. Add to the cream cheese and blend
well. Stir in the sugar, sultanas and egg yolks. Beat until well blended.
Whisk egg whites until stiff and fold into the mixture. Pour into the pastry
case.

Bake at 400°F, Gas Mark 6 for 25 minutes or until golden brown. Cool
and decorate with lemon slices. Serve chilled.
**Serves 4-6**

# Baked Plum and Walnut Cheesecake

**Base:**
4 oz. (1 cup) digestive biscuits
  (graham crackers), crushed
2 oz. (¼ cup) margarine, melted
1 oz. (¼ cup) walnuts, chopped
**Filling:**
8 oz. (1½ cups) plums, halved and
  stoned
8 oz. (1 cup) full fat soft cheese
5 fl. oz. (⅔ cup) natural
  (unflavored) yogurt

2 eggs, separated
2 oz. (¼ cup) castor (superfine)
  sugar
1 oz. (¼ cup) flour
½ teaspoon almond essence
**Topping:**
¼ pint (⅔ cup) soured cream
2 oz. (¼ cup) castor (superfine)
  sugar

Combine biscuits, margarine and walnuts and press into the base of a 9
inch loose bottomed tin. Place the plums, cut side up, on the base.

Blend the cream cheese with the yogurt, then beat in egg yolks, castor
sugar, flour and almond essence. Whisk egg whites until stiff and fold into
mixture. Pour over plums and bake at 350°F, Gas Mark 4 for 1 hour until
firm and beginning to brown. Reduce temperature to 300°F, Gas Mark 2.

Beat together the soured cream and sugar. Spread over the cheesecake
and bake for a further 15 minutes or until the topping has just set. Allow to
cool before removing from tin. Chill before serving.
**Serves 6-8**

# Russian Cheesecake

**Base:**
1½ oz. (3T) soft margarine,
  melted
3 oz. (¾ cup) digestive biscuits
  (graham crackers), crushed
**Filling:**
2 × 15 oz. cans black (bing)
  cherries
8 oz. (1 cup) full fat soft cheese

3 oz. (⅓ cup) castor (superfine)
  sugar
2 eggs, separated
2 oz. (½ cup) ground almonds
**Topping:**
1 tablespoon (1T) Kirsch
2 level teaspoons arrowroot
¼ pint (⅔ cup) juice from cherries

Mix margarine and biscuits and press mixture into the base of an 8 inch greased loose bottomed cake tin. Drain cherries and reserve juice. Arrange a layer of cherries over the biscuit base, reserving the remainder for decoration.

Soften the cheese and gradually add the sugar and egg yolks, beating thoroughly to avoid lumps. Stir in the ground almonds. Beat egg whites until stiff and fold into mixture. Pour into the tin and bake at 350°F, Gas Mark 4 for about 1 hour. Cool and remove from the tin.

Pour Kirsch over cheesecake and arrange remaining cherries on top. Blend arrowroot with a little cherry juice and heat the remainder until boiling. Add juice to arrowroot, stir and return to the pan. Heat, stirring until the glaze is clear and thickened. Pour over top and sides of cheesecake, brushing the sides to give an even coating. Serve chilled.
**Serves 6-8**

LEMON REFRIGERATED CHEESECAKE *(page 67)*, RUSSIAN
CHEESECAKE *(Photograph: Kraft Foods)*

# Italian Cheesecake

**Base:**
5 oz. (1¼ cups) plain (all-purpose)
  flour, sifted
2 oz. (¼ cup) sugar
½ teaspoon salt
½ teaspoon grated lemon rind
4 oz. (½ cup) butter
1 egg yolk
1½ tablespoons (2T) Amaretto di
  Saronno

**Filling:**
2 lb. (4 cups) Ricotta cheese
4 eggs
4 oz. (½ cup) sugar
1 oz. (¼ cup) flour
3 tablespoons (¼ cup) Amaretto
  di Saronno
1½ tablespoons (2T) raisins
1 tablespoon candied orange peel,
  chopped
1 tablespoon candied lemon peel,
  chopped

Place flour, sugar, salt and lemon peel in a bowl. Rub in butter until the mixture resembles fine breadcrumbs. Bind pastry with egg yolk and Amaretto di Saronno. Chill for 30 minutes. Roll out pastry to line a 9 inch flan dish. Bake 'blind' at 350°F, Gas Mark 4 for 15 minutes.

Place cheese in a bowl and blend in eggs, beating well. Add sugar, flour, Amaretto di Saronno, raisins and candied peel. Mix well. Pour into pastry case and bake at 325°F, Gas Mark 3 for 1 hour or until firm. Cool.

**Serves 8**

Amaretto di Saronno is an Italian liqueur made from a blend of apricots and cracked nut kernels infused in an eau de vie. If unobtainable, substitute apricot brandy.

# Baked Sultana Cheesecake

**Base:**
4 oz. (1 cup) plain (all-purpose)
  flour
2½ oz. (¼ cup + 1T) butter
½ oz. (1T) castor (superfine) sugar

**Filling:**
12 oz. (1½ cups) curd cheese
1 oz. (¼ cup) cornflour
  (cornstarch)
3 oz. (⅓ cup) castor (superfine)
  sugar
3 eggs, beaten
1½ teaspoons vanilla essence
¼ pint (⅔ cup) double (heavy)
  cream
2 oz. (⅓ cup) sultanas

**Topping:**
icing (confectioners') sugar, sifted

Sift the flour into a bowl and rub in the butter. Stir in the sugar and press this mixture over the base of an 8 inch tin. Bake at 375°F, Gas Mark 5 for 15 minutes.

Place cheese in a bowl and mix in the cornflour and sugar. Gradually beat in eggs with the vanilla essence and cream. Place sultanas in the pastry case and pour cheese mixture over. Bake at 350°F, Gas Mark 4 for ¾-1 hour until just firm in the centre. Leave to cool in the tin. Dredge with icing sugar before serving.

**Serves 8**

# Velvet Cheesecake

**Base:**

4 oz. (1 cup) self-raising flour,
  sifted
2½ oz. (¼ cup + 1T) butter
1 oz. (¼ cup) icing (confectioners')
  sugar
1 egg yolk

**Filling:**

8 oz. (1 cup) cottage cheese,
  sieved

1 oz. (¼ cup) ground almonds
½ lemon, grated rind and juice
½ teaspoon vanilla essence
½ oz. (1T) butter, softened
2 oz. (¼ cup) castor (superfine)
  sugar
2 oz. (⅓ cup) sultanas
2 eggs, separated

**Topping:**

1 egg white

Place flour in a bowl and rub in butter until the mixture resembles fine breadcrumbs. Stir in the icing sugar. Bind together with egg yolk and chill for 30 minutes.

Reserve one quarter of the pastry for a lattice topping. Roll the remainder to line a shallow 8 inch flan tin or dish.

Place the cottage cheese in a bowl and add the ground almonds, lemon rind, juice, vanilla essence, softened butter, sugar, sultanas and egg yolks. Mix until well blended. Whisk egg whites until stiff and fold into the mixture. Spoon into the pastry case and level with a knife.

Roll out remaining pastry and cut into ¼ inch strips. Arrange these in a lattice pattern over the cheesecake securing at the edges by dampening the pastry and pressing the strips down firmly.

Beat the egg white left from the pastry until frothy and use to brush over the surface of the pie. Bake at 350°F, Gas Mark 4 for 40 minutes or until golden. Serve warm.

**Serves 6-8**

# CHILLED FRUITY CHEESECAKES

## Blackcurrant Flavoured Cheesecake

**Base:**
*6 oz. (1½ cups) digestive biscuits
  (graham crackers), crushed*
*2 oz. (¼ cup) butter, melted*
**Filling:**
*4 tablespoons (⅓ cup)
  blackcurrant syrup*
*1 tablespoon water*
*½ oz. (1T) gelatine*
*8 oz. (1 cup) cottage cheese,
  sieved*

*4 oz. (½ cup) cream cheese*
*½ lemon, grated rind and juice*
*1 egg, separated*
*2 oz. (¼ cup) castor (superfine)
  sugar*
**Topping:**
*¼ pint (⅔ cup) double (heavy)
  cream*
*candied cake decorations*

Mix biscuits and butter and press into the base and sides of a greased 9 inch loose bottomed cake tin. Leave to set.

Place blackcurrant syrup and water in a pan and sprinkle gelatine over. Leave to soak for 5 minutes then heat gently until dissolved. Beat together the cottage cheese, cream cheese, lemon rind and juice. Whisk egg yolk with sugar until creamy and beat in the gelatine mixture. Combine with the cheeses, blending thoroughly. Whisk egg white until stiff and fold in. Pour into the flan case and chill until set.

Whip cream until thick and use to decorate cheesecake. Top with cake decorations. Serve chilled.
**Serves 4-6**

BLACKCURRANT FLAVOURED CHEESECAKE *(Photograph: Delrosa)*

# Creamy Pineapple Cheesecake

**Base:**
4 oz. (½ cup) butter
8 oz. (2 cups) digestive biscuits
  (graham crackers), crushed
**Filling:**
8 oz. can crushed pineapple
1 oz. (2T) gelatine
¼ pint (⅔ cup) evaporated milk
2 eggs, separated

4 oz. (½ cup) castor (superfine)
  sugar
1 lb. (2 cups) cottage cheese,
  sieved
1 lemon, grated rind and juice
**Topping:**
¼ pint (⅔ cup) double (heavy)
  cream

Melt butter and stir in the crushed digestive biscuits. Press into an 8 inch loose bottomed cake tin.

Drain pineapple and use juice to dissolve the gelatine. Whisk evaporated milk until thick and stir in the egg yolks and sugar. Whisk the egg whites until stiff and fold into the mixture with the cottage cheese, lemon rind and juice. Stir in about two thirds of the crushed pineapple and the dissolved gelatine. Pour onto the biscuit base and leave to set.

Whip cream until thick and use to decorate the cheesecake. Top with remaining pineapple.
**Serves 8-10**

# Cherry Cheesecake

**Base:**
3 oz. (¼ cup + 2T) butter
6 oz. (1½ cups) digestive biscuits
  (graham crackers), crushed
2 oz. (¼ cup) castor (superfine)
  sugar
**Filling:**
8 oz. (1 cup) cream cheese

½ pint (1¼ cups) double (heavy)
  cream
2 teaspoons gelatine
3 tablespoons (¼ cup) water
**Topping:**
15 oz. can cherry pie filling
½ oz. (2T) cornflour (cornstarch)

Melt the butter and mix with biscuits and sugar. Press into the base of a greased 8 inch loose bottomed cake tin. Leave to harden.

Mix the cream cheese and cream together. Dissolve gelatine in water in a bowl over a pan of hot water, then stir into the cheese mixture. Pour over biscuit base and leave in the refrigerator to set.

Place cherry pie filling in a pan and stir in the cornflour. Heat until thickened. Simmer for 1 minute and leave to cool slightly. Spoon over cheesecake and leave to set. Remove from the tin. Serve chilled.
**Serves 8**

# Redcurrant Cheesecake

**Base:**
3 oz. (⅓ cup) butter
3 tablespoons (¼ cup) golden
 (maple) syrup
6 oz. (4 cups) bran flakes
**Filling:**
2 eggs, separated
2 oz. (¼ cup) castor (superfine)
 sugar
8 oz. (1 cup) cream cheese

4 tablespoons (⅓ cup) lemon juice
½ oz. (1T) gelatine
2 tablespoons (3T) water
¼ pint (⅔ cup) double (heavy)
 cream, whipped
**Topping:**
4 tablespoons (⅓ cup) redcurrant
 jelly
8 oz. (2 cups) redcurrants, stewed
sugar to taste

Melt butter and golden syrup in a saucepan over low heat. Remove from the heat and stir in the bran flakes. Press into a greased 8 inch flan ring placed on a baking tray. Bake at 350°F, Gas Mark 4 for 10 minutes. Cool and remove flan ring.

Cream egg yolks and sugar together and beat into the cream cheese. Add lemon juice and continue beating until smooth. Dissolve gelatine in the water and blend into the cheese mixture. Leave until beginning to set, then fold in the whipped cream and stiffly beaten egg whites. Pour into the flan case and allow to set.

Melt redcurrant jelly and mix with the stewed redcurrants and sugar to taste. Spoon over the cheesecake and chill before serving.
**Serves 6**


# Banana Cheesecake

**Base:**
3 oz. (¼ cup + 2T) butter
8 oz. (2 cups) gingernuts
 (gingersnaps), crushed
**Filling:**
8 oz. (1 cup) cottage cheese,
 sieved
5 fl. oz. (⅔ cup) orange yogurt

2 tablespoons (3T) honey
2 bananas, mashed
juice of ½ lemon
2 teaspoons gelatine
4 tablespoons (⅓ cup) hot water
**Topping:**
¼ pint double (heavy) cream,
 whipped

Melt butter and mix with the biscuits. Press into an 8 inch fluted flan ring placed on a greased baking tray. Chill until firm.

Mix cottage cheese, yogurt, honey, bananas and lemon juice. Dissolve gelatine in hot water, allow to cool and stir into the mixture. Pour into the flan case and leave to set.

Decorate with whipped cream. Serve chilled.
**Serves 6**

# Peach Cheese Pie

**Base:**
4 oz. (½ cup) unsalted butter
1 tablespoon (1T) golden (maple)
  syrup
8 oz. (2 cups) digestive biscuits
  (graham crackers), crushed
**Filling:**
1 orange jelly (1 package orange
  flavored gelatin)

14½ oz. can sliced peaches
6 oz. (1½ cups) cream cheese
5 fl. oz. (⅔ cup) natural
  (unflavored) yogurt
1 egg, separated
**Topping:**
1 teaspoon arrowroot

Melt butter and syrup and stir in the biscuit crumbs. Press to the base and sides of an 8 inch spring form mould. Leave to cool.

Dissolve jelly in a little hot water and make up to ½ pint (1¼ cups) with juice from the peaches. Leave until beginning to thicken. Soften the cream cheese and beat in the yogurt and egg yolk until smooth. Whisk in the setting jelly. Whisk the egg white until stiff and fold in. When the mixture begins to set again pour into the biscuit base and leave in the refrigerator to set.

Remove the cheesecake from the tin. Arrange peach slices around the top edge of the cake. Blend arrowroot with a little water and make up to ¼ pint (⅔ cup) with water. Heat, stirring until the mixture clears and thickens. Cool and spoon over top of the cheesecake. Serve cold.
**Serves 6**

# Blackberry Cider Cheesecake

**Base:**
6 oz. (1½ cups) digestive biscuits
  (graham crackers), crushed
3 oz. (⅓ cup) butter, melted
**Filling:**
¼ pint (⅔ cup) cider
½ oz. (1T) gelatine
2 eggs, separated

2 oz. (¼ cup) castor (superfine)
  sugar
12 oz. (1½ cups) cream cheese
½ pint (1¼ cups) double (heavy)
  cream
**Topping:**
8 oz. (1¾ cups) blackberries
sugar to taste

Mix biscuits and butter and press into a greased 8 inch spring form cake tin. Chill.

Boil cider rapidly until reduced by about half. Cool a little then add the gelatine; stir until dissolved. Whisk together the egg yolks and sugar until creamy then fold in the cream cheese. Whip cream until thick and whisk egg whites until stiff. Fold both into the cheese mixture and pour into the cake tin. Leave to set. Remove the cheesecake from the tin.

Stew the blackberries with sugar until soft. Cool and blend or sieve to a purée. Spread over the cheesecake and chill.
**Serves 6-8**

PEACH CHEESE PIE *(Photograph: Cadbury Typhoo Food Advisory Service)*

# Quick Apricot Cheesecake

**Base:**
3 oz. (⅓ cup) butter
6 oz. (1½ cups) shortcake biscuits,
  crushed
**Filling:**
15 oz. can apricot halves

½ oz. (1T) gelatine
12 oz. (1½ cups) cream cheese
4 oz. (½ cup) castor (superfine)
  sugar
¼ pint (⅔ cup) soured cream

Melt butter and mix with the crushed shortcake biscuits. Press into the base of an 8 inch loose bottomed cake tin. Leave to set. Drain apricots and use a little of the juice to dissolve the gelatine. Reserve 5 apricot halves for decoration and chop the remainder.

Soften cream cheese and beat in the sugar and soured cream. Stir in the chopped apricots and dissolved gelatine. Spoon over the biscuit base and top with remaining apricot halves. Leave to set in the refrigerator.
**Serves 6**


# Strawberry Cheesecake

**Base:**
12 oz. (3 cups) digestive biscuits
  (graham crackers), crushed
6 oz. (¾ cup) butter, melted
3 oz. (⅓ cup) castor (superfine)
  sugar
**Filling:**
2 teaspoons gelatine
4 tablespoons (⅓ cup) water
3 eggs, separated
¼ pint (⅔ cup) milk
3 lemons, grated rind and juice

1 lb. (2 cups) cottage cheese
¼ pint (⅔ cup) double (heavy)
  cream, whipped
1 oz. (2T) castor (superfine) sugar
8 oz. (1½ cups) strawberries,
  sliced
**Topping:**
¼ pint (⅔ cup) double (heavy)
  cream
2 tablespoons (3T) milk
4 oz. (⅔ cup) small strawberries

Combine biscuits, butter and sugar and press into a 3 pint china flan dish, lining the base and sides. Dissolve gelatine in water over a low heat. Beat together the egg yolks and milk, stir in gelatine and heat without boiling. Remove from heat and add the lemon rind and 6 tablespoons (½ cup) lemon juice. Cool until beginning to set.

Combine the cooled mixture with the cottage cheese in an electric blender or whisk until smooth. Fold in the whipped cream.

Whisk egg whites until stiff and add the sugar. Fold into the cheese mixture. Spoon half the mixture into the biscuit case, cover with sliced strawberries then top with the remaining mixture. Chill.

For the topping, whip cream and milk together until thick. Decorate the pie with whirls of cream and strawberries. Serve chilled.
**Serves 8-10**

# Taunton Strawberry Cheesecake

**Base:**
8 oz. (2 cups) digestive biscuits
 (graham crackers), crushed
1½ oz. (3T) sugar
2 oz. (¼ cup) butter, melted
**Filling:**
½ oz. (1T) gelatine
¼ pint (⅔ cup) cider
¼ pint (⅔ cup) double (heavy)
 cream
¼ pint (⅔ cup) single (light) cream

8 oz. (1 cup) cottage cheese,
 sieved
1 tablespoon honey
4 oz. (1 cup) strawberries,
 chopped
**Topping:**
6 oz. (1¼ cups) strawberries,
 halved
castor (superfine) sugar to taste
¼ pint (⅔ cup) cider
1½ teaspoons arrowroot

Mix biscuits, sugar and butter together. Press into a greased 8 inch loose
bottomed cake tin. Leave to harden.

Dissolve the gelatine in 3 tablespoons (¼ cup) cider in a basin over a pan
of hot water. Stir in the remaining cider and leave to cool but not set. Whisk
double (heavy) and single (light) cream together. Fold in the cottage
cheese, honey and strawberries. Gradually add the cider mixture, stirring
thoroughly. Pour into the biscuit case and leave to set.

Place the halved strawberries in a bowl and sprinkle with sugar to taste
and cider. Leave for 2 hours.

Remove cheesecake from the tin. Drain the strawberries well, reserving
the cider and arrange strawberries on top of the cheesecake. Blend the
arrowroot with 2 tablespoons (3T) cider and heat the remaining cider.
Pour onto blended arrowroot, stirring constantly. Return to pan and heat,
stirring until clear and thickened. Cool slightly, then spoon over the
strawberries. Serve chilled.
**Serves 6-8**

# Hawaiian Delight

**Base:**
3 oz. (⅓ cup) butter
6 oz. (1½ cups) digestive biscuits
  (graham crackers), crushed
**Filling:**
4 teaspoons gelatine
6 tablespoons (½ cup) hot water
15 oz. can crushed pineapple,
  drained
1 tablespoon lemon juice

1½ oz. (3T) sugar
6 tablespoons (½ cup) double
  (heavy) cream
4 oz. (½ cup) cream cheese
**Topping:**
3 pineapple slices
glacé (candied) cherries
¼ pint (⅔ cup) double (heavy)
  cream, whipped

Melt butter and mix with the biscuits. Press into the base and sides of a greased 8 inch loose bottomed cake tin. Chill.

Dissolve the gelatine in hot water. Cool and blend with the crushed pineapple. Add lemon juice, sugar, cream and cheese. Stir until well blended and pour into the biscuit case. Leave to set. Remove from tin and decorate with pineapple slices, glacé cherries and whipped cream. Serve chilled.
**Serves 4**

# Grape Cheesecake

**Base:**
8 inch sponge cake, see page 54
**Filling:**
2 large eggs, separated
2 oz. (¼ cup) castor (superfine)
  sugar
½ oz. (1T) gelatine
8 oz. (1 cup) cream cheese

¼ pint (⅔ cup) single (light) cream
1 sachet Dream Topping
¼ pint (⅔ cup) milk
1 small lemon, grated rind and
  juice
**Topping:**
6 oz. (1 cup) grapes, halved and
  deseeded

Line an 8 inch loose bottomed tin with greaseproof (waxed) paper and place sponge cake in the tin.

Beat egg yolks and castor sugar until light and fluffy. Soften gelatine in 4 tablespoons (⅓ cup) water and place over a bowl of hot water to dissolve completely.

Add cream cheese and cream to egg yolk mixture and beat thoroughly. Stir in dissolved gelatine. Make up Dream Topping with milk as directed on the packet and fold into the mixture with the lemon rind and juice. Whisk egg whites until stiff and fold into the mixture. Pour over sponge cake and leave in a cold place to set.

Before serving ease the cheesecake away from the tin with a palette knife. Peel off greaseproof paper and place the cheesecake on a serving plate. Decorate with grapes. Serve chilled.
**Serves 6**

HAWAIIAN DELIGHT *(Photograph: Davis Gelatine)*

# Pear and Cinnamon Cheesecake

**Base:**
2 oz. (¼ cup) margarine
4 oz. (1 cup) sweet biscuits,
  crushed
½ oz. (1T) brown sugar
¼ teaspoon cinnamon
**Filling:**
2 small oranges
12 oz. (1½ cups) cream cheese

2 large eggs, separated
3 oz. (⅓ cup) castor (superfine)
  sugar
¼ pint (⅔ cup) double (heavy)
  cream
½ oz. (1T) gelatine
**Topping:**
8 oz. can pears, drained and sliced

Melt the margarine and mix with the biscuits, brown sugar and cinnamon. Press into an 8 inch dish or tin. Leave to set.

Remove peel and pith from 1 orange and cut the flesh into segments. Arrange over the biscuit base. Grate rind from the other orange and beat with the cream cheese. Beat egg yolks with 1½ oz. (3T) castor sugar until light and fluffy. Squeeze the juice from the second orange and beat into the egg yolks with the cream cheese. Whisk egg whites until stiff and then whisk in the remaining sugar. Whip cream until thick. Dissolve the gelatine in 2 tablespoons (3T) water. Fold egg whites and cream into the cheese mixture with the dissolved gelatine. Pour over biscuit base and leave in a cold place to set.

Decorate with sliced pears.

**Serves 6-8**

# Blackcurrant Topped Cheesecake

**Base:**
4 oz. (1 cup) digestive biscuits
  (graham crackers), crushed
1 oz. (½ cup) wheatgerm
2 oz. (¼ cup) butter, melted

**Filling:**
8 oz. (1 cup) cream cheese
4 oz. (½ cup) cottage cheese
3 oz. (⅓ cup) castor (superfine)
  sugar

½ oz. (1T) gelatine
3 tablespoons (¼ cup) hot water
2-3 drops vanilla essence
¼ pint (⅔ cup) double (heavy)
  cream, whipped
3 egg whites, stiffly beaten

**Topping:**
1 tablespoon (1T) cornflour
  (cornstarch)
15 oz. can blackcurrants

Mix biscuits, wheatgerm and butter together and press into a greased 8 inch loose bottomed cake tin. Leave to set.

Beat cream cheese, cottage cheese and sugar together. Dissolve gelatine in hot water and combine with the cheese and vanilla essence. Fold in whipped cream and stiffly beaten egg whites. Pour mixture into cake tin and refrigerate for at least 3 hours.

Blend cornflour (cornstarch) with a little blackcurrant juice in a saucepan. Add remainder of juice and fruit and heat, stirring until the mixture thickens. Cool and spread over the cheesecake. Serve chilled.

**Serves 8**

# Pineapple and Cherry Cheesecake

**Base:**
6 oz. shortcrust pastry (basic pie dough), see page 11
**Filling:**
¼ pint (⅔ cup) milk
2 eggs, separated
4 oz. (½ cup) castor (superfine) sugar
8 oz. can pineapple rings
½ pineapple jelly (½ package pineapple flavored gelatin)
8 oz. (1 cup) cottage cheese, sieved
grated rind of ½ lemon
¼ pint (⅔ cup) double (heavy) cream
**Topping:**
2-3 pineapple rings, halved
glacé (candied) cherries

Roll out pastry to line an 8-9 inch flan ring placed on a baking tray. Bake 'blind' at 375°F, Gas Mark 5 for 20 minutes. Cool and remove ring.

Gently heat the milk, egg yolks and sugar until the custard thickens, but do not boil. Drain the pineapple, reserving the juice.

Dissolve jelly in the pineapple juice and stir into the custard with the cheese and grated lemon rind. Set aside to cool. Whip cream until thick and fold into the mixture when just beginning to set. Whisk egg whites until stiff and fold in. Pour into pastry case and leave to set. Decorate with the pineapple pieces and glacé cherries.
**Serves 6**

# Apricot and Almond Cheesecake

**Base:**
3 oz. (⅓ cup) butter
8 oz. (2 cups) macaroons, crushed
**Filling:**
5 fl. oz. (⅔ cup) natural (unflavored) yogurt
8 oz. (1 cup) cottage cheese, sieved
4 tablespoons (⅓ cup) apricot jam
½ teaspoon vanilla essence
2 teaspoons gelatine
**Topping:**
15 oz. can apricot halves, drained
5 angelica diamonds

Melt butter and stir in the crushed macaroons. Press into an 8 inch ovenproof pie dish to line the base and sides. Bake at 375°F, Gas Mark 5 for 10 minutes. Cool.

Beat together the yogurt, cottage cheese, 3 tablespoons (¼ cup) jam and vanilla essence. Dissolve gelatine in a little water and stir into the mixture until well blended. When on the point of setting, quickly pour into the almond crust and leave in a cool place to set.

Decorate the cheesecake with apricot halves and angelica. Heat remaining jam with 1 tablespoon water. Spoon over the apricots.
**Serves 6**

STRAWBERRY CREAM CHEESE FLAN *(page 46)*, PLAIN CHOCOLATE CHEESECAKE *(page 84)*, APRICOT AND ALMOND CHEESECAKE, PINEAPPLE AND CHERRY CHEESECAKE
*(Photograph: Cadbury Food Advisory Service)*

# Strawberry Cream Cheese Flan

**Base:**
8 oz. (2 cups) plain (all-purpose)
  flour
8 oz. (1 cup) butter
3 tablespoons (¼ cup) single
  (light) cream
**Filling:**
15 oz. can strawberries

1 oz. (¼ cup) cornflour
  (cornstarch)
1 oz. (2T) castor (superfine) sugar
**Topping:**
3 oz. (⅓ cup) cream cheese
¼ pint (⅔ cup) double (heavy)
  cream

Sift flour into a bowl and rub in butter until the mixture resembles fine breadcrumbs. Mix to a stiff dough with the cream. Wrap in aluminium foil and chill for 1 hour.

Roll out on a floured surface and use to line a 9 inch flan ring placed on a baking tray. Prick base and bake 'blind' at 400°F, Gas Mark 6 for 25 minutes. Reduce to 325°F, Gas Mark 3 for a further 15 minutes or until cooked through. Remove flan ring and cool on a wire tray.

Place strawberries in a saucepan. Blend cornflour and sugar with a little water and stir into the strawberries. Heat, stirring until the mixture thickens. Cool slightly and pour into the pastry case. Leave until cold.

Soften the cream cheese. Whip the cream until thick then mix with the cheese. Spread or pipe the cream mixture over the strawberries. Serve chilled.
**Serves 6**

# Pineapple Flower Cheesecake

**Base:**
4 oz. (1 cup) ginger biscuits,
  crushed
2 oz. (¼ cup) butter, melted
**Filling:**
¼ pint (⅔ cup) milk
2 eggs, separated
4 oz. (½ cup) castor (superfine)
  sugar

8 oz. can pineapple pieces
1 pineapple jelly (1 package
  pineapple flavored gelatin)
12 oz. (1½ cups) cottage cheese
¼ pint (⅔ cup) double (heavy)
  cream
**Topping:**
angelica
glacé (candied) cherries

Mix biscuits with melted butter and press into an 8 inch loose bottomed cake tin.

Heat the milk, egg yolks and sugar until the custard thickens, stirring continuously. Do not allow to boil. Drain pineapple and reserve the fruit for decoration. Dissolve the jelly in the pineapple syrup. Place cottage cheese in a bowl and gradually stir in the custard and jelly. Leave until almost set.

Whip the cream until thick and fold into the pineapple mixture. Whisk the egg whites until stiff and fold in gently. Pour over biscuit base and chill until firm.

Remove cheesecake from cake tin and place on a serving plate. Decorate the top with pineapple pieces, making a flower design. Use angelica strips for the stalks and cherries for the flower centres. Remaining fruit can be arranged around the edge of the dish.
**Serves 8**

# Blackcurrant Cheese Flan

**Base:**
3 oz. (⅓ cup) butter
6 oz. (1½ cups) digestive biscuits
  (graham crackers), crushed
**Filling:**
1 oz. (¼ cup) cornflour
  (cornstarch)
1 oz. (2T) castor (superfine) sugar

½ pint (1¼ cups) milk
10 fl. oz. (1¼ cups) blackcurrant
  yogurt
8 oz. (1 cup) cottage cheese
7½ oz. can blackcurrants, drained
**Topping:**
¼ pint (⅔ cup) double (heavy)
  cream, whipped

Melt butter and mix with biscuit crumbs. Press into a shallow 8 inch flan dish and leave to harden.

Blend cornflour and sugar with a little milk. Heat remaining milk and pour onto the blended mixture. Stir and return to the pan. Heat, stirring continuously until the sauce thickens.

Cool slightly and stir in the yogurt and cottage cheese. Add the blackcurrants, reserving a few for decoration. Pour into the flan case. Chill in the refrigerator.

Decorate with blackcurrants and whipped cream. Serve chilled.
**Serves 6**
Decorate the cheesecake with sprigs of fresh blackcurrants, if available.

# Peach Yogurt Cheesecake

**Base:**
8 oz. (2 cups) digestive biscuits
  (graham crackers), crushed
4 oz. (½ cup) butter, melted
**Filling:**
4 teaspoons gelatine
¼ pint (⅔ cup) hot water
12 oz. (1½ cups) cream cheese
5 fl. oz. (⅔ cup) peach yogurt

1 tablespoon lemon juice
3 eggs, separated
pinch of salt
8 oz. (1 cup) castor (superfine)
  sugar
½ pint (1¼ cups) double (heavy)
  cream
**Topping:**
15 oz. can sliced peaches

Mix biscuits with melted butter and press into an 8 inch loose bottomed cake tin.

Dissolve gelatine in the hot water. Beat the cream cheese, peach yogurt and lemon juice until smooth. Place egg yolks, salt, 5 oz. (⅔ cup) sugar in a saucepan and cook over a low heat for a few minutes. Stir occasionally. When thickened remove from the heat and add the dissolved gelatine. Mix well and leave to cool until thickened.

Beat in the peach cheese mixture. Whisk the egg whites with the remaining sugar until stiff. Whip the cream until thick. Fold egg whites and cream into the cheese mixture and pour into the biscuit case. Chill for about 4 hours until set. Remove cheesecake from the tin and decorate with peach slices.
**Serves 8**

BLACKCURRANT CHEESE FLAN *(Photograph: Milk Marketing Board)*

# Raspberry Peach Cheesecake

**Base:**
2 oz. (¼ cup) butter
4 oz. (1 cup) plain (all-purpose)
  flour
1 oz. (2T) castor (superfine) sugar
1 egg yolk
**Filling:**
3 eggs, separated
4 oz. (½ cup) castor (superfine)
  sugar
½ lemon, grated rind and juice
¼ pint (⅔ cup) soured cream
12 oz. (1½ cups) cottage cheese,
  sieved
½ oz. (1T) gelatine
2 tablespoons (3T) warm water
**Topping:**
¼ pint (⅔ cup) double (heavy)
  cream, whipped
1 oz. (¼ cup) flaked almonds,
  browned
3 large peaches, sliced
juice of ½ lemon
8 oz. (1½ cups) raspberries

Rub butter into flour until the mixture resembles fine breadcrumbs. Add the sugar. Mix egg yolk with 1-2 teaspoons water. Add to the rubbed in mixture and work to a stiff dough. Knead lightly and chill for 30 minutes.

Roll out pastry to line an 8 inch loose bottomed cake tin. Prick the base and bake 'blind' at 375°F, Gas Mark 5 for 15-20 minutes. Leave to cool in the tin.

Whisk the egg yolks and sugar together over hot water until thick and creamy. Remove from heat and stir in lemon juice, rind, soured cream and cottage cheese. Dissolve gelatine in the warm water and fold into mixture.

Whisk egg whites until stiff and fold into the cheese mixture. Pour mixture into the pastry case and leave in a cool place to set.

Remove cheesecake from tin and coat the sides with whipped cream. Press on browned almonds. Sprinkle peach slices with lemon juice and arrange on top of cheesecake with raspberries. Chill before serving.
**Serves 8**

# Viennoise Cheesecake

**Base:**
2½ oz. (⅔ cup) self-raising flour
pinch of salt
2 oz. (¼ cup) butter
1 oz. (2T) castor (superfine) sugar
2-3 drops vanilla essence
**Filling:**
8 oz. (1 cup) full fat soft cheese
¼ pint (⅔ cup) soured cream
2 eggs, separated
3 oz. (⅓ cup) castor (superfine)
  sugar

grated rind of ½ lemon
½ oz. (1T) gelatine
4 tablespoons (⅓ cup) water
¼ pint (⅔ cup) double (heavy)
  cream
**Topping:**
8 oz. plums, poached
2 tablespoons (3T) redcurrant jelly
2 teaspoons arrowroot
1 tablespoon (1T) water

Sift flour and salt into a bowl. Beat the butter with sugar and vanilla until light and fluffy. Stir in the flour. Spread mixture over the base of an 8 inch spring form mould and flatten with a dampened fork. Bake at 375°F, Gas Mark 5 for 10 minutes. Allow to cool.

Beat the cream cheese until smooth and stir in the soured cream. Beat the egg yolks, sugar and lemon rind in a bowl over a pan of hot water until thick and pale in colour. Stir into the cheese mixture.

Soften the gelatine in the water in a basin placed over a pan of hot water. Stir until dissolved. Allow to cool and then add to the cheese mixture. Whip the cream lightly and fold into the mixture. Whisk the egg whites until stiff and fold in. Stir the mixture gently over iced water until it begins to thicken. Pour over the cheesecake base and smooth the top. Refrigerate until set.

Reserve ½ pint (1¼ cups) juice from the poached plums. Dissolve the redcurrant jelly in the plum juice. Blend arrowroot with water and add to the pan. Heat, stirring until the glaze is thickened and boiling. Carefully stir in the fruit. Leave to cool then spoon over the cheesecake. Serve chilled.
**Serves 8**

# Harvest Cheesecake

**Base:**
2 oz. (½ cup) digestive biscuits
  (graham crackers), crushed
2 oz. (½ cup) muesli
2 oz. (¼ cup) soft margarine,
  melted
1 oz. (2T) castor (superfine) sugar

**Filling:**
8 oz. (1 cup) full fat soft cheese
3 oz. (⅓ cup) castor (superfine)
  sugar
2 eggs, separated

5 fl. oz. (⅔ cup) lemon yogurt
½ lemon, grated rind and juice
½ oz. (1T) gelatine
4 tablespoons (⅓ cup) water
¼ pint (⅔ cup) double (heavy)
  cream
2 oz. (⅓ cup) sultanas

**Topping:**
1 dessert apple, cored and sliced
2 tablespoons (3T) honey
4 oz. (1 cup) seedless grapes
walnut halves

Mix biscuits and cereal with melted margarine and stir in the sugar. Press into an 8 inch greased loose bottomed cake tin. Leave to harden.

Cream the cheese and sugar until smooth and gradually add the egg yolks, yogurt, lemon rind and juice. Dissolve gelatine in the water placed in a basin over a pan of hot water. Cool and add to the cheese mixture, blending thoroughly. Whip the cream lightly and whisk the egg whites until stiff. Fold both into the mixture until well blended. Stir in the sultanas and pour mixture onto the crumb base. Chill until firm.

Remove the tin but leave the cheesecake on the base. Poach the apple slices gently in the honey until soft. Cool completely. Reserve the honey. Decorate the cheesecake with grapes, nuts and sliced apple. Brush with honey. Serve cold.

**Serves 8**

**Variation:**
Replace lemon yogurt with natural (unflavored) yogurt and add 2 teaspoons honey to the filling. The cream can also be omitted to give a lighter cheesecake.

HARVEST CHEESECAKE *(Photograph: Kraft Foods)*

# Honey and Banana Cheesecake

**Sponge cake base:**
4 oz. (½ cup) soft margarine
4 oz. (½ cup) castor (superfine)
  sugar
2 eggs, beaten
4 oz. (1 cup) self-raising flour
**Filling:**
2 tablespoons (3T) clear honey
½ oz. (1T) gelatine

2 tablespoons (3T) water
8 oz. (1 cup) cream cheese
2 eggs, separated
¼ pint (⅔ cup) soured cream
3 oz. (⅓ cup) castor (superfine)
  sugar
**Topping:**
1 banana
juice of ½ lemon

Cream the margarine and sugar until light and fluffy. Add the eggs gradually, beating thoroughly after each addition. Fold in the flour, using a metal spoon.

Spread the mixture into a greased and lined 8 inch cake tin. Bake at 375°F, Gas Mark 5 for 25-30 minutes until well risen and golden. Turn out and cool on a wire rack. Place the sponge cake in an 8 inch china flan dish and spread with honey.

Soften gelatine in cold water in a bowl and place over a pan of hot water until completely dissolved. Place cream cheese, egg yolks and soured cream in a bowl and beat thoroughly. Whisk egg whites until stiff and add the castor sugar a little at a time. Fold into the cream cheese mixture. Gradually stir in the dissolved gelatine and mix well. Pour over sponge base and leave to set.

Just before serving, peel the banana and slice thinly. Dip banana slices in lemon juice before arranging on top of the cheesecake.
**Serves 6**

# Pineapple Mint Cheesecake

**Base:**
4 oz. (1 cup) digestive biscuits
  (graham crackers), crushed
1 oz. (2T) castor (superfine) sugar
1 oz. (2T) butter, melted
**Filling:**
8 oz. can pineapple rings
½ oz. (1T) gelatine
1 lb. (2 cups) cottage cheese,
  sieved

2 lemons, juice and grated rind
4 oz. (½ cup) castor (superfine)
  sugar
2 eggs, separated
¼ pint (⅔ cup) double (heavy)
  cream
**Decoration:**
fresh sprigs mint

Mix biscuits, sugar and melted butter and press into an 8 inch loose bottomed cake tin.

Drain pineapple juice into a large bowl and sprinkle with gelatine. Reserve 1 pineapple slice for decoration and chop the remainder finely.

Mix together the pineapple, cottage cheese, lemon juice and rind. Heat gelatine and pineapple juice in a bowl over a pan of hot water until dissolved. Beat in the sugar and egg yolks. Heat until the mixture is the consistency of pouring cream. Remove from the heat and allow to cool. When thickened but not set blend into the cheese mixture. Beat egg whites and fold into the mixture.

Whip cream until thick and gently fold in. Pour over biscuit base in the tin and chill until set. Remove from tin. Decorate with remaining pineapple and sprigs of fresh mint.
**Serves 8**

# CHILLED CITRUS CHEESECAKES

## Mandarin and Cherry Cheesecake

**Base:**
8 oz. (2 cups) digestive biscuits
  (graham crackers), crushed
4 oz. (½ cup) butter, melted
**Filling:**
4 teaspoons gelatine
¼ pint (⅔ cup) hot water
12 oz. (1½ cups) cream cheese
5 fl. oz. (⅔ cup) natural
  (unflavored) yogurt
2 tablespoons (3T) lemon juice
3 eggs, separated
8 oz. (1 cup) sugar
¼ pint (⅔ cup) double (heavy)
  cream, whipped
**Topping:**
11 oz. can mandarin oranges,
  drained
15 oz. can cherries, drained

Mix biscuits with melted butter and press into the base and sides of an 8 inch loose bottomed cake tin.

Dissolve gelatine in hot water. Blend cream cheese, yogurt and lemon juice until smooth. Beat egg yolks with 5 oz. (⅔ cup) sugar until white and creamy. Stir in dissolved gelatine and cheese mixture. Mix well. Whisk egg whites with remaining sugar until stiff. Fold into the mixture with the whipped cream. Pour into prepared crumb base.

Chill for about 4 hours until firm. Decorate with mandarins and cherries before serving.
**Serves 8**

MANDARIN AND CHERRY CHEESECAKE *(Photograph: Davis Gelatine)*

# Mandarin and Grape Cheesecake

**Base:**
2 oz. (¼ cup) unsalted butter
3 oz. (3 cups) cornflakes, crushed
1 oz. (2T) sugar
**Filling:**
½ oz. (1T) gelatine
8 oz. (1 cup) cottage cheese, sieved
4 oz. (½ cup) cream cheese
1 lemon, grated rind and juice
2 eggs, separated

pinch of salt
3 oz. (⅓ cup) castor (superfine) sugar
¼ pint (⅔ cup) double (heavy) cream
**Topping:**
black grapes, halved and deseeded
11 oz. can mandarin oranges, drained

Melt butter and mix with cornflakes and sugar. Press into the base of a loose bottomed 8 inch cake tin. Leave to set in the refrigerator.

Soften the gelatine in 3 tablespoons (¼ cup) cold water in a bowl. Place over a pan of hot water to dissolve. Mix cottage cheese, cream cheese and lemon rind. Beat egg yolks with salt and half the sugar until light and fluffy. Add lemon juice to dissolved gelatine and gradually whisk into the egg yolks. Blend with the cheese mixture.

Whisk egg whites until stiff and whisk in the remaining sugar. Whip cream lightly and fold into the cheese mixture with the egg whites. Pour over prepared base and chill until firm.

Remove the cake tin and place on a serving plate. Decorate with black grapes and mandarin oranges.
**Serves 6**

# Grapefruit Cheesecake

**Base:**
3 oz. (⅓ cup) butter
3 tablespoons (¼ cup) golden
 (maple) syrup
6 oz. (5 cups) bran flakes
**Filling:**
½ oz. (1T) gelatine
2 tablespoons (3T) water

8 oz. (1 cup) cottage cheese,
 sieved
¼ pint (⅔ cup) double (heavy)
 cream
juice of 1 grapefruit
1 oz. (2T) sugar
**Topping:**
grapefruit segments

Melt butter and golden syrup and stir in the bran flakes. Mix well and press into an 8 inch flan dish reserving a little for decoration. Bake at 350°F, Gas Mark 4 for 10 minutes. Cool.

Dissolve gelatine in water in a bowl over a pan of hot water. Mix together the cottage cheese, cream, grapefruit juice and sugar. Whisk in the cooled gelatine and when thick turn the mixture into the flan case. Leave to set.

Decorate with grapefruit segments and remaining bran flake mixture before serving.
**Serves 6**

# Black Grape and Grapefruit Cheesecake

½ oz. (1T) gelatine
3 tablespoons (¼ cup) water
8 oz. (1 cup) cottage cheese,
 sieved
5 fl. oz. (⅔ cup) natural
 (unflavored) yogurt

2 grapefruit
8 oz. (2 cups) black grapes
2 egg whites
2 oz. (¼ cup) castor (superfine)
 sugar

Dissolve gelatine in the water in a basin over a pan of hot water. Leave to cool. Mix cottage cheese with yogurt and blend in the gelatine. Grate rind and squeeze the juice from 1 grapefruit. Remove pips from half of the grapes and chop roughly, then add to the cheese mixture with the grapefruit juice and rind. Whisk egg whites until stiff and whisk in the sugar. Fold into cheese mixture and pour into a dampened 8 inch cake tin. Leave in the refrigerator to set.

Remove cheesecake from tin and place on a serving plate. Peel and segment the remaining grapefruit. Halve the reserved grapes and remove the pips. Use to decorate the cheesecake. Serve chilled.
**Serves 6**

# Slimmer's Citrus Grape Cheesecake

**Base:**
1 oz. (2T) butter
5 low calorie digestive biscuits
 (graham crackers), crushed

**Filling:**
½ lime jelly (½ package lime
 flavored gelatin)
6 tablet sweeteners

¼ pint (⅔ cup) hot water
grated rind of 1 lemon
8 oz. (1 cup) cottage cheese,
 sieved

**Topping:**
3 tablespoons (¼ cup) lemon juice
1 ½ teaspoons arrowroot
halved grapes to decorate

Melt butter and mix with biscuits. Press to the base of an 8 inch flan dish or ring. Chill. Dissolve jelly and tablet sweeteners in hot water and leave to cool. Beat lemon rind into cottage cheese then combine with the jelly. Pour over biscuit base and leave in refrigerator to set.

Make lemon juice up to ¼ pint (⅔ cup) with water. Blend arrowroot with a little of this, then pour into a pan with the remaining liquid. Heat, stirring until the mixture clears. Cool. Decorate cheesecake with grapes and spoon the glaze over. Serve chilled.

**Serves 4-6**


# Country Cheesecake

**Base:**
1 ½ oz. (3T) butter
1 tablespoon (1T) golden (maple)
 syrup
4 oz. (1 cup) muesli

**Filling:**
6 oz. (¾ cup) cream cheese
½ pint (1 ¼ cups) double (heavy)
 cream

½ oz. (1T) gelatine
½ pint (1 ¼ cups) orange juice
1 large orange, peeled and
 chopped

**Topping:**
1 large orange, segmented
angelica leaves

Melt butter and syrup and mix with the muesli. Press into the base of a greased 8 inch loose bottomed cake tin. Leave to set.

Beat cream cheese until soft and gradually stir in the cream. Whisk until the mixture thickens. Dissolve gelatine in 4 tablespoons (⅓ cup) warmed orange juice and add to the mixture with remaining orange juice. Stir the chopped fruit into the mixture. When beginning to set pour into the tin and chill until firm.

Remove cheesecake from tin and decorate with orange segments and angelica leaves. Serve chilled.

**Serves 6-8**

SLIMMER'S CITRUS GRAPE CHEESECAKE *(Photograph: Energen Foods)*

# Mandarin Cheddar Cheesecake

3 eggs, separated
3 oz. (⅓ cup) castor (superfine)
  sugar
11 oz. can mandarin oranges
½ oz. (1T) gelatine
8 oz. (2 cups) Cheddar cheese,
  grated

¼ pint (⅔ cup) milk
¼ pint (⅔ cup) single (light) cream
¼ pint (⅔ cup) double (heavy)
  cream

Whisk egg yolks and sugar together in a basin over hot water until thickened. Drain mandarins and add half the juice to the egg yolks. Use remainder to dissolve the gelatine.

Mix cheese and milk together. Whip the creams together until thick. Fold into the egg yolk mixture with the grated cheese and gelatine. Chop half the mandarin oranges and stir into the mixture. Whisk egg whites until stiff and fold into the cheesecake mixture. Pour into a greased and lined 8 inch square cake tin. Refrigerate until set. Turn out and decorate with remaining mandarins.
**Serves 6**

# Walnut and Orange Cheesecake

**Base:**
2 oz. (¼ cup) butter
4 oz. (1 cup) digestive biscuits
  (graham crackers), crushed
1 oz. (2T) brown sugar
¼ teaspoon cinnamon
**Filling:**
1 large orange

¼ pint (⅔ cup) double (heavy)
  cream
5 fl. oz. (⅔ cup) mandarin yogurt
3 oz. (⅓ cup) cream cheese
2 oz. (¼ cup) castor (superfine)
  sugar
**Topping:**
6 walnut halves

Melt the butter and mix with the crushed biscuits, sugar and cinnamon. Press into an 8 inch flan ring placed on a serving plate. Leave to harden.

Peel orange, removing all the pith. Carefully segment the orange, reserving 6 pieces for decoration. Chop remainder finely, drain and arrange over biscuit base.

Whip the cream until thick and fold in the yogurt. Cream the cheese and sugar together and mix with the cream and yogurt. Pour over the oranges and chill until firm. Decorate with orange segments and walnut halves.
**Serves 4-6**

# Fluffy Orange and Lemon Cheesecake

**Base:**
4 oz. (1 cup) digestive biscuits
  (graham crackers), crushed
1 oz. (2T) brown sugar
2 oz. (¼ cup) butter, melted
**Filling:**
2 eggs, separated
4 oz. (½ cup) castor (superfine)
  sugar
1 orange, grated rind and juice
1 lemon, grated rind and juice
½ oz. (1T) gelatine
2 tablespoons (3T) cold water
12 oz. (1½ cups) cottage cheese,
  sieved
¼ pint (⅔ cup) soured cream
**Topping:**
6 tablespoons (½ cup) double
  (heavy) cream, whipped
1 orange, peeled and segmented

Combine biscuits, brown sugar and butter. Mix well and press into a greased 8 inch loose bottomed cake tin.

Beat egg yolks with 2 oz. (¼ cup) castor sugar. Stir in the citrus juice and rind. Place the bowl over a pan of hot water and stir until the mixture thickens enough to coat the back of a spoon. Soften gelatine in cold water and stir into the mixture until dissolved. Leave to cool.

Add cottage cheese and soured cream and mix thoroughly. Whisk egg whites until just stiff and fold in the remaining sugar. Fold gently into the cheese mixture and pour over the biscuit base. Leave in a cool place to set.

Turn onto a serving plate and decorate with fresh whipped cream and orange slices.
**Serves 8**

# Lemon Cheese Flan

**Base:**
8 inch sponge cake, see page 54
**Filling:**
3 tablespoons (¼ cup) raspberry
  jam
8 oz. (1 cup) cream cheese
2 oz. (¼ cup) castor (superfine)
  sugar
grated rind of 1 lemon
1 tablespoon lemon juice
**Topping:**
black grapes
½ lemon, sliced

Place sponge cake in an 8 inch flan dish and spread with jam. Cream together the cheese and sugar until well blended. Stir in the lemon rind and juice. Spread over the jam and top with grapes and lemon slices.

Serve chilled.
**Serves 4-6**

# Tangy Lemon Cheesecake

**Base:**
4 oz. (1 cup) digestive biscuits
  (graham crackers), crushed
2 oz. (¼ cup) butter, melted
2 oz. (¼ cup) sugar
**Filling:**
1 lemon jelly (1 package lemon
  flavored gelatin)

½ pint (1¼ cups) water
1 lb. (2 cups) cream cheese
1 packet Dream Topping
¼ pint (⅔ cup) milk
juice of 1 lemon
**Topping:**
15 oz. can cherry pie filling

Mix biscuits, butter and sugar and press into the base of a greased 8 inch loose bottomed cake tin. Chill until firm.

Make up the jelly with water and leave until beginning to set. Soften the cheese and gradually blend in the jelly. Make up the Dream Topping with the milk as directed on the packet. Whisk into the cheese and jelly mixture with the lemon juice. Pour onto crumb base and leave until set.

Remove cheesecake from tin. Spread the cherry pie filling around the top edge of the cake to decorate. Serve chilled.
**Serves 8**


# Sunshine Cheesecake

**Base:**
6 oz. (1½ cups) digestive biscuits
  (graham crackers), crushed
1 oz. (2T) sugar
1½ oz. (3T) butter, melted
**Filling:**
½ oz. (1T) gelatine
⅓ pint (1 cup) orange juice
¼ pint (⅔ cup) double (heavy)
  cream

¼ pint (⅔ cup) single (light) cream
8 oz. (1 cup) cottage cheese,
  sieved
1 tablespoon clear honey
2 oz. (⅓ cup) sultanas
**Topping:**
crystallized (candied) orange slices

Mix biscuits, sugar and melted butter. Press into the base of an 8 inch loose bottomed cake tin. Leave to set.

Dissolve gelatine in 3 tablespoons (¼ cup) orange juice in a basin over a pan of hot water. Add the remaining orange juice.

Whip the creams together until thick. Add cottage cheese, honey and sultanas; mix well. Gradually blend in the orange juice and mix thoroughly. Pour over the biscuit base and leave in a cool place until set. Remove cheesecake from tin and decorate with crystallized orange slices.
**Serves 6-8**

TANGY LEMON CHEESECAKE *(Photograph: Bird's Products)*

# Glazed Lemon Cheesecake

**Base:**
3 oz. (⅓ cup) butter
6 oz. (1½ cups) sweet biscuits,
   crushed
2 oz. (¼ cup) castor (superfine)
   sugar
**Filling:**
½ lemon jelly (½ package lemon
   flavored gelatin)

8 oz. (1 cup) soft cream cheese
2 oz. (¼ cup) castor (superfine)
   sugar
grated rind of 1 lemon
**Topping:**
3 tablespoons (¼ cup) lemon juice
1½ teaspoons arrowroot
1 oz. (2T) castor (superfine) sugar
knob of butter

Melt butter and mix with biscuits and sugar. Press into an 8 inch flan dish. Leave to set.

Place jelly in a measuring jug and make up to ¼ pint (⅔ cup) with hot water. Stir until dissolved then chill in the refrigerator until just beginning to set.

Blend cream cheese with sugar and lemon rind. Gradually beat in the jelly. Spoon the mixture into the biscuit base and chill until set.

Make lemon juice up to ¼ pint (⅔ cup) with water. Blend arrowroot with a little of this liquid. Add remainder of the liquid and sugar. Heat, stirring until the mixture boils. Continue boiling until the glaze is clear. Remove from heat and add a knob of butter. Cool until lukewarm, then spoon over the filling. Chill thoroughly before serving.
**Serves 4-6**


# Almond and Orange Cheesecake

**Base:**
3 oz. (⅓ cup) butter
6 oz. (1½ cups) digestive biscuits
   (graham crackers), crushed
1 teaspoon almond essence
½ oz. (1T) castor (superfine) sugar
**Filling:**
¼ pint (⅔ cup) double (heavy)
   cream

8 oz. (1 cup) cottage cheese,
   sieved
2 tablespoons (3T) natural
   (unflavored) yogurt
2 tablespoons (3T) clear honey
1 teaspoon lemon juice
**Topping:**
1 orange, thinly sliced

Melt butter and stir in the biscuits, almond essence and sugar. Mix well and press into the base of an 8 inch flan dish. Leave to harden.

Whip cream until stiff and fold in cottage cheese, yogurt, honey and lemon juice. Spread over biscuit base and chill until firm. Decorate with orange slices. Serve chilled.
**Serves 6**

# Lemon Refrigerated Cheesecake

**Base:**
2 oz. (¼ cup) soft margarine
2 oz. (¼ cup) castor (superfine)
   sugar
1 tablespoon golden (maple)
   syrup
1½ oz. (⅓ cup) roasted hazelnuts
   (filberts), chopped
2 oz. (2 cups) puffed rice cereal
**Filling:**
8 oz. (1 cup) full fat soft cream
   cheese

3 oz. (⅓ cup) castor (superfine)
   sugar
2 eggs, separated
5 fl. oz. (⅔ cup) lemon yogurt
½ lemon, juice and grated rind
½ oz. (1T) gelatine
4 tablespoons (⅓ cup) water
¼ pint (⅔ cup) double (heavy)
   cream, whipped
2 oz. (⅓ cup) sultanas
**Topping:**
½ oz. (½ cup) puffed rice cereal

Melt margarine, sugar and syrup in a pan and stir in the nuts and puffed rice cereal. Mix well and press into the base of a greased 8 inch loose bottomed cake tin. Leave to harden.

Cream cheese and sugar together until smooth. Gradually add the egg yolks, lemon yogurt, lemon juice and rind. Beat thoroughly. Dissolve gelatine in the water in a bowl over a pan of hot water. Cool slightly and add to the cheese mixture. Whisk the egg whites until stiff. Whip the cream and fold into the cheese mixture with the stiffly beaten egg whites and sultanas.

Pour into the tin and chill until firm. Remove cheesecake from tin and serve on the base decorated with puffed rice cereal.
**Serves 8-10**
**Variation:**
Substitute the puffed rice with a biscuit crumb base (see page 66). Make the filling as above. Pipe cream rosettes around the edge of the cheesecake and top with mimosa balls and angelica leaves. Complete the decoration with lemon twists. To make these, cut several lemon slices through the centre then twist the two halves in opposite directions. Arrange lemon twists on top of the cheesecake.

# Lemon Oat Cheesecake

**Base:**
1½ oz. (3T) margarine
3 oz. (1 cup) porridge oats
1 oz. (2T) sugar
**Filling:**
1 lemon jelly (1 package lemon
 flavored gelatin)
½ pint (1¼ cups) water
1 lb. (2 cups) cream cheese

4 oz. (½ cup) castor (superfine)
 sugar
grated rind of 1 lemon
**Topping:**
3 tablespoons (¼ cup) lemon juice
1½ teaspoons arrowroot
2 oz. (2 squares) plain
 (semi-sweet) chocolate

Melt margarine and mix with oats and sugar. Press into the base of a greased 8 inch tin with removable base. Chill until firm.

Dissolve jelly in water and leave to cool. Beat cream cheese with sugar and lemon rind until smooth. When the jelly is just beginning to set, mix a little at a time into the cheese mixture. Pour into the tin and leave to set.

Make the lemon juice up to ¼ pint (⅔ cup) with water and blend the arrowroot with a little of this liquid. Place in a pan with the remaining liquid and heat, stirring until the mixture thickens and clears. Cool slightly. Remove cheesecake from tin and top with the glaze.

Melt the chocolate in a bowl over a pan of hot water. Spread the melted chocolate thinly on a laminated surface and leave until almost set. Then, using the edge of a palette knife shave off pieces of chocolate to form flakes. Decorate the top edge of the cake with the chocolate flakes. Serve chilled.
**Serves 8-10**

# Quick Lemon Cheesecake

**Base:**
6 oz. (1½ cups) digestive biscuits
 (graham crackers), crushed
3 oz. (⅓ cup) butter, melted

**Filling:**
¼ pint (⅔ cup) double (heavy)
 cream
1 lemon, grated rind and juice
8 oz. (1 cup) cottage cheese
2 oz. (¼ cup) castor (superfine)
 sugar

Mix crumbs with the melted butter. Press half this mixture into the base of an 8 inch flan ring placed on a serving plate. Chill until firm.

Whip cream until thick and fold in the lemon rind, juice, cottage cheese and sugar. Spread over the base and chill until firm. Remove flan ring and top cheesecake with the remaining crumbs, forming a lattice pattern. Serve chilled.
**Serves 4-6**

LEMON OAT CHEESECAKE *(Photograph: Scott's Porridge Oats)*

# Orange Cheesecake

**Base:**
4 oz. (1 cup) digestive biscuits
  (graham crackers), crushed
2 oz. (¼ cup) castor (superfine)
  sugar
2 oz. (¼ cup) butter, melted
**Filling:**
3 oranges
juice of 1 lemon
2 tablespoons (3T) gelatine
2 eggs, separated

½ pint (1¼ cups) milk
3 oz. (⅓ cup) castor (superfine)
  sugar
1¼ lb. (2½ cups) cottage cheese,
  sieved
¼ pint (⅔ cup) double (heavy)
  cream, whipped
**Topping:**
3 oranges, peeled and segmented
¼ pint (⅔ cup) double (heavy)
  cream

Mix biscuits, sugar and butter and press into a greased 9 inch loose bottomed cake tin.

Finely grate the rind of 2 oranges and squeeze the juice from 3 oranges. Combine the orange juice with the lemon juice. Pour 4 tablespoons (⅓ cup) of citrus juice into a cup and sprinkle the gelatine over.

Whisk together the egg yolks, milk and 2oz. (¼ cup) sugar. Place in a pan and heat gently without boiling for a few minutes. Add gelatine and stir constantly until dissolved. Leave to cool until just beginning to set, then add the orange rind and 6 tablespoons (½ cup) citrus juice.

Beat cottage cheese into the jelly mixture. Whisk egg whites until stiff then whisk in the remaining sugar. Fold into the citrus mixture with the whipped cream. Pour over the biscuit base and chill until set.

Remove cheesecake from tin. Arrange orange segments around the edge, overlapping them slightly. Decorate with whipped cream.
**Serves 8**

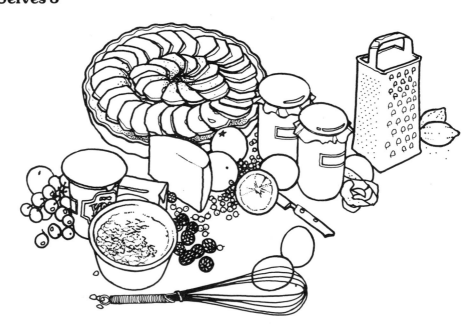

# Mandarin and Lemon Cheesecake

**Base:**
4 oz. (1 cup) digestive biscuits
  (graham crackers), crushed
2 oz. (¼ cup) butter, melted
**Filling:**
8 oz. (1 cup) cream cheese
5 fl. oz. (⅔ cup) natural
  (unflavored) yogurt
1 lemon jelly (1 package lemon
  flavored gelatin)

3 tablespoons (¼ cup) water
1 lemon, grated rind and juice
2 oz. (¼ cup) sugar
**Topping:**
11 oz. can mandarin oranges,
  drained
6 tablespoons (½ cup) double
  (heavy) cream, whipped

Mix crushed biscuits and melted butter and press into an 8 inch flan ring.

Mix the cream cheese and yogurt together. Dissolve the lemon jelly in the water over a low heat. When cool, add the lemon rind, juice and sugar. Add to the cheese and yogurt mixture and whisk until smooth. Pour over biscuit base and leave in a cool place to set.

Before serving decorate with mandarin oranges and whipped cream.
**Serves 6**

# Marmalade Cheesecake

**Base:**
2 oz. (¼ cup) butter
4 oz. (1 cup) digestive biscuits
  (graham crackers), crushed
1 oz. (⅓ cup) roasted hazelnuts
  (filberts), ground
**Filling:**
3 eggs, separated
6 oz. (¾ cup) castor (superfine)
  sugar

8 oz. (1 cup) cream cheese
2 tablespoons (3T) lemon juice
3 tablespoons (¼ cup) fine cut
  marmalade
½ oz. (1T) gelatine
3 tablespoons (¼ cup) water
¼ pint (⅔ cup) double (heavy)
  cream
**Topping:**
rind from marmalade

Melt butter and mix with the biscuits and ground hazelnuts (filberts). Press into the base of a greased 8 inch loose bottomed cake tin. Leave to harden.

Beat together the egg yolks and sugar. Add the cream cheese and continue beating until the mixture is thick and creamy. Stir in the lemon juice and marmalade. Dissolve gelatine in water and add to the mixture. Whip cream until thick and whisk egg whites until stiff. Fold both into the cream cheese mixture, blending well. Pour into tin and leave to set.

Remove cheesecake from tin and decorate with rind from the marmalade.
**Serves 8**

# NUTTY CHEESECAKES

## Hazelnut Cheesecake

**Base:**
2 oz. (¼ cup) butter
4 oz. (1 cup) digestive biscuits
  (graham crackers), crushed
1 oz. (2T) brown sugar
**Filling:**
3 oz. (⅓ cup) cream cheese
2 oz. (¼ cup) castor (superfine)
  sugar
¼ pint (⅔ cup) double (heavy)
  cream

5 fl. oz. (⅔ cup) hazelnut (filbert)
  yogurt
**Topping:**
¼ pint (⅔ cup) double (heavy)
  cream, whipped
2 oz. (⅓ cup) hazelnuts (filberts),
  skinned and toasted
1 chocolate flake, crushed

Melt the butter and mix with biscuit crumbs and brown sugar. Press into an 8 inch flan ring on a serving plate. Leave to harden.

Soften cheese and beat in sugar. Whip cream lightly and stir in the yogurt. Blend with cream cheese mixture and spoon into the biscuit base. Chill in refrigerator until firm. Remove the flan ring.

Decorate the cheesecake with cream rosettes and toasted hazelnuts. Sprinkle chocolate flake in the centre and serve chilled.
**Serves 6-8**

## Nut and Vanilla Cheesecake

**Base:**
2 oz. (¼ cup) butter
4 oz. (1 cup) digestive biscuits
  (graham crackers), crushed
**Filling:**
½ oz. (1T) gelatine
4 tablespoons (⅓ cup) hot water
3 oz. (⅓ cup) castor (superfine)
  sugar

¼ teaspoon salt
2 eggs, separated
¼ pint (⅔ cup) double (heavy)
  cream
2 teaspoons vanilla essence
8 oz. (1 cup) cream cheese
**Topping:**
chopped nuts

Melt butter and mix with the biscuits. Press into an 8 inch flan dish. Chill.

Dissolve gelatine in water. Place sugar, salt, egg yolks and half the cream in a saucepan. Heat, stirring until the mixture thickens slightly. Remove from heat and beat in vanilla essence and dissolved gelatine. Gradually blend in the cheese. Leave until beginning to thicken.

Whisk egg whites until stiff. Whip remaining cream until thick and fold both into the cheese mixture. Pour into crumb base and chill until set. Top with chopped nuts.
**Serves 6**

HAZELNUT CHEESECAKE *(Photograph: National Dairy Council)*

# Nutty Citrus Cheesecake

**Base:**
2 oz. (¼ cup) butter
2 oz. (¼ cup) brown sugar
1 tablespoon (1T) golden (maple)
  syrup
1 oz. (¼ cup) hazelnuts (filberts),
  chopped
2 oz. (2 cups) puffed rice cereal
**Filling:**
2 eggs, separated
6 oz. (¾ cup) cream cheese
¼ pint (⅔ cup) double (heavy)
  cream
grated rind of 1 lemon

6¼ oz. can frozen concentrated·
  orange juice
4 oz. (½ cup) castor (superfine)
  sugar
½ oz. (1T) gelatine
3 tablespoons (¼ cup) water
**Topping:**
2 oz. (¼ cup) sugar
½ oz. (1T) gelatine
¼ pint (⅔ cup) water
juice of 1 lemon
1 oz. (¼ cup) hazelnuts (filberts),
  chopped

Melt butter, sugar and syrup together and stir in the nuts and puffed rice.
Mix well and press into the base of a greased 8 inch loose bottomed cake
tin. Leave to set.

Beat egg yolks and cheese together until smooth. Whip cream until
thick. Blend into cheese mixture with the lemon rind and half the orange
juice concentrate. Whisk egg whites until stiff then whisk in the sugar a little
at a time. Dissolve gelatine in water and whisk into the egg whites, then fold
this into the cream mixture. Pour over the base and allow to set.

For the topping, dissolve sugar and gelatine in the water over a low heat.
Make remaining orange juice concentrate up to ½ pint (1¼ cups) with
water and add to the gelatine with the lemon juice. When beginning to set
pour over cheesecake and chill until firm. Remove from tin. Decorate with
chopped nuts and serve chilled.
**Serves 8**

74

# Almond and Honey Cheesecake

**Base:**
8 oz. (2 cups) macaroons, crushed
3 oz. (⅓ cup) butter, melted
**Filling:**
5 fl. oz. (⅔ cup) natural
  (unflavored) yogurt
8 oz. (1 cup) cottage cheese,
  sieved
1 tablespoon clear honey

½ teaspoon vanilla essence
grated rind of 1 orange
grated rind of 1 lemon
**Decoration:**
3 crystallized (candied) orange
  slices
1 oz. (¼ cup) blanched almonds,
  toasted

Combine the crushed macaroons and butter and press into an 8 inch pie plate. Chill until very firm.

Place yogurt, cottage cheese, honey, vanilla essence, orange and lemon rind in a bowl and beat well. Spoon into the flan case and refrigerate for at least 1 hour. Decorate with crystallized orange slices and toasted almonds. Serve chilled.
**Serves 4-6**

# Coconut Cheesecake

**Base:**
3 oz. (⅓ cup) margarine
6 oz. (1½ cups) coconut biscuits,
  crushed
¼ teaspoon mixed spice
**Filling:**
½ oz. (1T) gelatine
3 tablespoons (¼ cup) water
12 oz. (1½ cups) cream cheese

1 lemon, grated rind and juice
2 eggs, separated
3 oz. (⅓ cup) castor (superfine)
  sugar
¼ pint (⅔ cup) double (heavy)
  cream
**Topping:**
1 oz. (⅓ cup) desiccated
  (shredded) coconut

Melt margarine and mix with crushed biscuits and mixed spice. Press into an 8 inch flan dish.

Soften gelatine in cold water and place over a bowl of hot water until completely dissolved. Soften cream cheese and stir in the lemon rind. Beat egg yolks with half the sugar until light and fluffy. Beat into the cream cheese with the lemon juice.

Whisk egg whites until stiff and fold in remaining sugar. Whip cream until stiff. Fold egg whites and cream into the cheese mixture. Stir in dissolved gelatine and mix thoroughly. Pour over biscuit base and leave to set.

Toast coconut and sprinkle over the cheesecake to decorate.
**Serves 8**

# Cottage Crunch Flan

**Base:**
2 oz. (¼ cup) butter
5 oz. (1¼ cups) digestive biscuits
  (graham crackers), crushed
**Filling:**
1 tablespoon custard powder
½ pint (1¼ cups) milk

2 oz. (¼ cup) sugar
8 oz. (1 cup) cottage cheese
2 oz. (⅓ cup) sultanas
1 oz. (3T) mixed (candied) peel
1 oz. (¼ cup) walnuts, chopped
**Topping:**
grated nutmeg

Melt butter and mix with the crushed biscuits. Press into the base and sides of an 8 inch flan dish. Leave to harden.

Blend custard powder with a little cold milk and half the sugar. Heat remaining milk and add to the custard, stirring. Return to the pan and heat, stirring until the mixture thickens. Leave to cool.

Add remaining sugar to the cottage cheese with the sultanas, mixed peel and walnuts. Stir in the cool custard, blending well. Spoon into crumb case and sprinkle the cheesecake with grated nutmeg. Chill until firm.
**Serves 4-6**


# Hazelnut Crunch Cheesecake

**Base:**
2 oz. (¼ cup) margarine
2 oz. (¼ cup) castor (superfine)
  sugar
1 tablespoon golden (maple)
  syrup
1½ oz. (¼ cup) roasted hazelnuts
  (filberts), chopped
2 oz. (2 cups) puffed rice cereal
**Filling:**
8 oz. (1 cup) full fat cream cheese
2 eggs, separated

5 fl. oz. (⅔ cup) hazelnut (filbert)
  yogurt
½ oz. (1T) gelatine
4 tablespoons (⅓ cup) water
3 oz. (⅓ cup) castor (superfine)
  sugar
**Topping:**
¼ pint (⅔ cup) double (heavy)
  cream, whipped
2 oz. (⅓ cup) roasted hazelnuts
  (filberts)

Melt margarine with sugar and golden syrup. Stir in hazelnuts (filberts) and puffed rice cereal. Mix well and press into a greased 8 inch loose bottomed cake tin. Leave to cool and harden.

Soften cheese and gradually beat in the egg yolks and yogurt. Dissolve gelatine in the water in a bowl placed over a pan of hot water. Add to the cheese mixture. Whisk egg whites until stiff and then whisk in the sugar. Fold into the cheese mixture and pour over prepared base. Chill until firm. Remove from tin and decorate with whipped cream and hazelnuts.
**Serves 8-10**

COTTAGE CRUNCH FLAN *(Photograph: Milk Marketing Board)*

# German Cheesecake

**Base:**
6 oz. (1 ½ cups) plain (all-purpose)
  flour
1 oz. (¼ cup) baking powder
4 oz. (½ cup) butter
2 oz. (¼ cup) sugar
2 egg yolks
1 tablespoon (1T) rum
**Filling:**
1 ½ lb. (3 cups) Quark cheese
½ pint (1 ¼ cups) milk
¼ pint (⅔ cup) double (heavy)
  cream
1 lemon, grated rind and juice
juice of 1 orange
4 oz. (¾ cup) raisins
4 oz. (½ cup) sugar
1 oz. (2T) gelatine
**Topping:**
2 tablespoons (3T) apricot jam
1 oz. (¼ cup) flaked almonds,
  toasted

Sift flour and baking powder into a bowl and rub in butter until the mixture resembles fine breadcrumbs. Stir in the sugar and bind with egg yolks and rum. Chill in refrigerator for 1 hour. Roll out to line a 10 inch flan tin. Bake 'blind' at 375°F, Gas Mark 5 for 15-20 minutes.

Place Quark, milk, cream, lemon rind, juice, orange juice, raisins and sugar in a basin and mix well. Soften gelatine in cold water in a bowl. Place over a pan of hot water until dissolved. Mix into the cheese mixture. Pour into the pastry case and leave in a cold place to set.

Warm apricot jam and sieve to remove any lumps. Brush over top and sides of the cheesecake. Press flaked almonds to the sides.
**Serves 10**

# Almond Cheesecake

**Base:**
1 oz. (2T) butter
1 oz. (2T) brown sugar
2 teaspoons golden (maple) syrup
6 oz. (1 ½ cups) digestive biscuits
  (graham crackers), crushed
**Filling:**
1 oz. (¼ cup) blanched almonds,
  chopped
8 oz. (1 cup) cottage cheese,
  sieved
¼ pint (⅔ cup) double (heavy)
  cream, whipped
1 teaspoon grated orange rind
½ teaspoon almond essence
2 oz. (¼ cup) castor (superfine)
  sugar
**Topping:**
1 oz. (¼ cup) blanched almonds,
  toasted

Melt butter, brown sugar and syrup and mix with the biscuits. Press into the base of an 8 inch flan ring on a serving plate. Leave to harden. Sprinkle chopped almonds over the base.

Mix cottage cheese, whipped cream, orange rind, almond essence and sugar. Blend thoroughly. Spoon over the chopped almonds. Chill until firm and remove the flan ring. Before serving, sprinkle with toasted almonds.
**Serves 6**

# Walnut Mint Cheesecake

**Base:**

1½ oz. (3T) margarine

4 oz. (1 cup) chocolate digestive
  biscuits (graham crackers),
  crushed

2 oz. (½ cup) walnuts, chopped

**Filling:**

8 oz. (1 cup) full fat cream cheese

4 oz. (½ cup) castor (superfine)
  sugar

1½ teaspoons vanilla essence

1½ teaspoons peppermint
  essence

4 oz. (4 squares) plain
  (semi-sweet) chocolate

½ oz. (1T) gelatine

8 fl. oz. (1 cup) water

¼ pint (⅔ cup) double (heavy)
  cream

**Topping:**

¼ pint (⅔ cup) double (heavy)
  cream, whipped

walnut halves to decorate

Melt margarine and mix with biscuits and walnuts. Press into a greased 8 inch loose bottomed cake tin. Bake at 350°F, Gas Mark 4 for 10 minutes. Allow to cool.

Place cheese in a bowl and blend in the sugar, vanilla essence and peppermint essence. Beat thoroughly. Melt chocolate in a basin over hot water and add to the cheese mixture.

Dissolve gelatine in the water in a basin over hot water. Add to mixture, stirring. Whip cream until thick and carefully fold in, blending thoroughly. Pour over biscuit base and chill until firm.

Decorate with whipped cream and walnut halves.

**Serves 8**

# CHEESECAKES WITH A DIFFERENCE

## Chocolime Cheesecake

**Base:**
4 oz. (1 cup) digestive biscuits
  (graham crackers), crushed
2 oz. (¼ cup) butter, melted
**Filling:**
1 tablespoon cornflour
  (cornstarch)
1 tablespoon cocoa powder
1 tablespoon castor (superfine)
  sugar
½ pint (1¼ cups) milk

2 eggs, separated
6 oz. (¾ cup) cream cheese
1 lime jelly (1 package lime
  flavored gelatin)
4 tablespoons (⅓ cup) water
5 fl. oz. (⅔ cup) natural
  (unflavored) yogurt
**Topping:**
chocolate buttons
glacé (candied) cherries

Mix biscuits and butter together. Press into the base of a greased 8 inch loose bottomed cake tin. Leave to harden.

Blend the cornflour, cocoa and sugar with a little of the cold milk. Heat remaining milk, pour onto cocoa then return to the pan. Heat, stirring until the chocolate custard thickens. Cool slightly and beat in the egg yolks and cream cheese.

Dissolve the jelly in the water and beat into the mixture with the yogurt. Leave in a cool place until beginning to set. Whisk egg whites until stiff and fold into mixture. Pour over biscuit base and leave in refrigerator to set. Remove from tin and decorate with chocolate buttons and glacé cherries.
**Serves 6-8**

PINEAPPLE FLOWER CHEESECAKE *(page 47)*, CHOCOLIME
CHEESECAKE *(Photograph: Cadbury Food Advisory Service)*

# Baked Chocolate Orange Cheesecake

**Base:**
2 oz. (½ cup) plain tea biscuits,
  crushed
2 teaspoons castor (superfine)
  sugar
pinch of cinnamon
pinch of grated nutmeg
**Filling:**
3 eggs
5 oz. (⅔ cup) castor (superfine)
  sugar

12 oz. (1½ cups) full fat cream
  cheese
1½ oz. (⅓ cup) plain (all-purpose)
  flour
4 oz. (4 squares) plain
  (semi-sweet) chocolate
**Topping:**
¼ pint (⅔ cup) double (heavy)
  cream, whipped
1 fresh orange, peeled and
  segmented

Mix biscuits with sugar, cinnammon and nutmeg. Sprinkle over the sides and base of a greased 8 inch loose bottomed cake tin. Secure a band of aluminium foil around the outside of the tin so that it comes 1 inch above the rim.

Whisk eggs and sugar together until thick. Blend cream cheese and flour together until smooth. Melt chocolate in a basin over hot water and when cool add to the cheese mixture. Gradually add the whisked eggs and beat thoroughly. Pour into tin and bake at 350°F, Gas Mark 4 for approximately 1 hour.

Remove the foil and allow the cake to cool a little before removing from the tin. When cold, fill the hollow with whipped cream and decorate with orange segments.
**Serves 8-10**

# Chocolate and Strawberry Cheesecake

**Base:**
6 oz. ( ¾ cup) butter
2 oz. (2 squares) chocolate
8 oz. (2 cups) digestive biscuits
 (graham crackers), crushed
**Filling:**
1 tablespoon brandy
12 oz. (2¼ cups) strawberries,
 halved
½ oz. (1T) gelatine
¼ pint (⅔ cup) hot water

1 lb. (2 cups) cream cheese
2 tablespoons (3T) lemon juice
3 eggs, separated
4 oz. ( ½ cup) castor (superfine)
 sugar
2 teaspoons grated lemon rind
pinch of salt
½ pint (1¼ cups) double (heavy)
 cream
**Topping:**
4 oz. (1 cup) whole strawberries

Melt butter and chocolate in a basin over hot water. Mix with the biscuit crumbs. Press to the base and sides of a chilled 8 inch spring form mould. Chill.

Sprinkle brandy over the halved strawberries and set aside. Dissolve gelatine in the hot water and allow to cool. Blend the cream cheese with the lemon juice.

Place beaten egg yolks, sugar, lemon rind and ¼ pint (⅔ cup) water in a basin over a pan of hot water. Cook until thickened, stirring occasionally. While still warm, add to the cheese, beating until very smooth. Add gelatine and salt then chill until thickened.

Whip cream lightly and fold into the mixture. Stiffly whip the egg whites and fold into the mixture with the brandied strawberry halves. Pour mixture into crumb case and refrigerate for at least 6 hours. Before serving decorate with whole strawberries.
**Serves 8-10**

# Chocolate Cheesecake

**Base:**
3 oz. (¼ cup + 2T) butter
6 oz. (1½ cups) digestive biscuits
  (graham crackers), crushed
**Filling:**
½ pint (1¼ cups) milk
1 packet chocolate instant dessert

8 oz. (1 cup) cottage cheese,
  sieved
4 tablespoons (⅓ cup) double
  (heavy) cream
**Topping:**
2 oz. (2 squares) milk (sweet)
  chocolate, grated

Melt the butter and mix with biscuits. Press into the base of an 8 inch flan ring on a serving plate. Leave to harden.

Pour milk into a basin. Sprinkle on the instant dessert and whisk until thick. Stir in the cottage cheese. Whip cream until thick and fold in. Spoon mixture over cheesecake base and chill until firm. Remove the flan ring and decorate with grated chocolate. Serve chilled.
**Serves 6**

# Plain Chocolate Cheesecake

**Base:**
4 oz. (½ cup) butter, melted
1 oz. (2T) castor (superfine) sugar
7 oz. (1¾ cups) digestive biscuits
  (graham crackers), crushed
2 oz. (2 squares) plain
  (semi-sweet) chocolate
**Filling:**
8 oz. (1 cup) cream cheese

2 tablespoons (3T) lemon juice
1 egg, separated
1 oz. (2T) castor (superfine) sugar
¼ pint (⅔ cup) milk
½ teaspoon grated lemon rind
½ oz. (1T) gelatine
**Topping:**
1½ oz. (1½ squares) plain
  (semi-sweet) chocolate

Mix butter, sugar and biscuits together and press into a greased 8 inch spring form mould. Melt the chocolate in a bowl over a pan of hot water and spread over the biscuit base. Leave to harden.

Beat cream cheese with lemon juice until smooth. Place egg yolk, sugar and milk in a saucepan and beat well. Heat gently until thick enough to coat the back of a spoon, but do not boil. Gradually stir in the cheese and grated lemon rind. Dissolve gelatine in a little warm water and add to the mixture. Whisk egg white until stiff and fold in. Pour onto biscuit base and leave to set.

Decorate with flakes of chocolate (see Lemon Oat Cheesecake, page 68).
**Serves 6-8**
Alternatively, decorate with lemon twists and piped melted chocolate (as illustrated on page 45).

# Ginger Cheesecake

**Base:**
2 oz. ( ¼ cup) soft margarine
1 ½ oz. (3T) demerara (raw) sugar
4 oz. (1 cup) gingernuts
  (gingersnaps), crushed

**Filling:**
8 oz. (1 cup) full fat soft cheese
2 eggs, separated
5 fl. oz. ( ⅔ cup) natural
  (unflavored) yogurt

2 pieces stem (preserved) ginger
½ oz. (1T) gelatine
5 tablespoons (6T) water
1 tablespoon ginger syrup
2 oz. ( ¼ cup) sugar

**Topping:**
¼ pint ( ⅔ cup) double (heavy)
  cream, whipped
stem (preserved) ginger

Melt margarine and sugar, then mix with biscuits. Press into the base of a greased 8 inch loose bottomed cake tin. Leave to harden.

Soften the cheese and gradually beat in the egg yolks and yogurt. Rinse excess syrup from the ginger with boiling water and chop finely. Dissolve gelatine in the water over a pan of hot water and add to the cheese mixture blending thoroughly.

Whisk egg whites until stiff and fold in the ginger syrup and sugar. Carefully fold into the cheese mixture. Pour into cake tin and smooth the surface. Chill until firm.

Remove the cheesecake from the tin but leave on the base. Decorate with whipped cream and pieces of stem ginger.
**Serves 6-8**

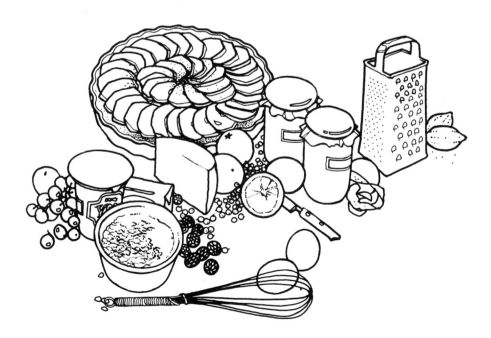

# Jamaican Cheesecake

**Base:**
2 oz. (¼ cup) soft margarine
2 oz. (¼ cup) brown sugar
4 oz. (1 cup) oatmeal biscuits,
  crushed
½ teaspoon ground ginger
**Filling:**
4 oz. (¾ cup) raisins
4 tablespoons (⅓ cup) rum
8 oz. (1 cup) full fat soft cheese

2 eggs, separated
¼ pint (⅔ cup) soured cream
½ oz. (1T) gelatine
4 tablespoons (⅓ cup) water
3 oz. (⅓ cup) castor (superfine)
  sugar
**Topping:**
¼ pint (⅔ cup) double (heavy)
  cream, whipped

Melt margarine and sugar together and mix with the biscuits and ground ginger. Press into a greased 8 inch loose bottomed cake tin. Leave to harden.

Place raisins in a bowl, add the rum and leave to soak. Soften the cheese and beat in the egg yolks and soured cream. Dissolve gelatine in the water in a bowl over a pan of hot water. Stir into the cheese mixture. Whisk egg whites until stiff and whisk in the sugar. Fold into the mixture with the raisins and rum. Pour onto biscuit base and chill until firm. Remove from tin and decorate with whirls of cream.
**Serves 6-8**

# Lemon and Ginger Cheesecake

**Base:**
3 oz. (⅓ cup) butter
1 oz. (2T) brown sugar
6 oz. (1½ cups) gingernuts
  (gingersnaps), crushed
**Filling:**
4 oz. (½ cup) cream cheese

4 oz. (½ cup) castor (superfine)
  sugar
2 eggs, separated
½ pint (1¼ cups) double (heavy)
  cream
2 lemons

Melt the butter and sugar in a pan and stir in biscuit crumbs. Mix well and press to the base and sides of an 8 inch pie plate. Chill.

Beat cream cheese and sugar together thoroughly, then beat in egg yolks. Whip cream until it stands in soft peaks and fold into the cheese mixture. Grate the rind from 1 lemon and squeeze the juice from both and add to the mixture. Whisk the egg whites until stiff and fold in. Pour into the crumb case and bake at 350°F, Gas Mark 4 for about 50 minutes until the filling has set. Allow to cool and chill before serving.
**Serves 8**

# Vanilla Cheesecake

**Base:**
2 oz. (¼ cup) butter
1 oz. (2T) sugar
6 oz. (1½ cups) digestive biscuits
  (graham crackers), crushed

**Filling:**
½ oz. (1T) gelatine
3 tablespoons (¼ cup) water
2 eggs, separated

½ pint (1¼ cups) milk
1 oz. (2T) castor (superfine) sugar
2 teaspoons vanilla essence
12 oz. (1½ cups) curd cheese,
  softened

**Topping:**
fresh strawberries, halved
  (optional)

Melt butter and sugar and mix with biscuits. Press half the mixture into the base of a greased 8 inch loose bottomed cake tin. Leave to harden.

Place the gelatine and water in a bowl over a pan of hot water. Stir until dissolved. Put the egg yolks, milk, sugar and vanilla essence in a bowl. Cook over a pan of simmering water until the mixture coats the back of a spoon. Chill. Stir in the curd cheese and gelatine. Whisk egg whites until stiff and fold in evenly. Pour mixture over biscuit base and cover with remaining crumbs. Leave in refrigerator for several hours to set.

Remove the tin and arrange the strawberries on the cheesecake.

**Serves 6-8**

# Coffee Meringue Cheesecake

**Base:**
2 egg whites
pinch of cream of tartar
4 oz. (½ cup) castor (superfine)
  sugar
1 oz. (¼ cup) walnuts, finely
  chopped

**Filling:**
2 oz. (¼ cup) castor (superfine)
  sugar
½ oz. (1T) gelatine

2 egg yolks
¼ pint (⅔ cup) milk
1 tablespoon coffee essence
  (strong black coffee)
8 oz. (1 cup) cream cheese
¼ pint (⅔ cup) double (heavy)
  cream

**Topping:**
¼ pint (⅔ cup) double (heavy)
  cream, whipped
8-12 walnut halves

Beat egg whites with cream of tartar until stiff. Beat in half the sugar then fold in the remainder with the chopped walnuts. Spread over the base and sides of a buttered 8 inch flan dish. Bake at 275°F, Gas Mark 1 for 1-1½ hours until lightly brown and crisp throughout. Cool.

Place sugar, gelatine, egg yolks, milk and coffee essence in a bowl. Cook over a pan of simmering water until the mixture coats the back of a spoon. Cool. Beat cream cheese until soft then blend in the coffee sauce. Whip cream lightly and fold in. Pour into meringue case and leave to set.

Decorate with whipped cream and walnut halves.

**Serves 8-12**

*VANILLA CHEESECAKE (Photograph: Ambrosia Custard)*

# Coffee and Brandy Cheesecake

**Base:**
2 oz. (¼ cup) soft margarine
2½ oz. (¼ cup + 1T) castor
  (superfine) sugar
2 tablespoons (3T) golden
  (maple) syrup
4 oz. (1 cup) digestive biscuits
  (graham crackers), crushed
2 oz. (½ cup) walnuts, chopped
**Filling:**
8 oz. (1 cup) full fat soft cheese
2 eggs, separated
¼ pint (⅔ cup) soured cream
½ oz. (1T) gelatine

4 tablespoons (⅓ cup) water
3 oz. (⅓ cup) castor (superfine)
  sugar
1 tablespoon brandy
**Topping:**
2 teaspoons coffee essence
  (strong black coffee)
½ pint (1¼ cups) water
½ oz. (1T) gelatine
2 oz. (¼ cup) castor (superfine)
  sugar
whipped cream (optional)
walnuts (optional)

Melt margarine, sugar and syrup together and mix with the biscuits and chopped walnuts. Press into the base of a greased 8 inch loose bottomed cake tin. Leave to harden.

Soften cheese and beat in the egg yolks and soured cream. Dissolve gelatine in water in a basin over a pan of hot water and add to the cheese mixture. Whisk egg whites until stiff and fold in the sugar. Fold carefully into the cheese mixture with the brandy. Pour onto crumb base and leave to set.

For the topping, mix the coffee essence and water together. Dissolve gelatine in half the liquid and stir in the sugar until dissolved. Add remaining liquid and leave to thicken. Carefully pour over the setting filling. Cool until firm, then remove from the tin. Decorate with whipped cream and walnuts, if desired.

**Serves 8**

# INDEX

# INDEX

PDO 80-333